Experiencing God's Story of Life and Hope

Experiencing God's Story of Life and Hope

A Workbook for Spiritual Formation

J. Scott Duvall

Kregel
Academic & Professional

Experiencing God's Story of Life and Hope: A Workbook for Spiritual Formation

© 2008 by J. Scott Duvall

Published by Kregel Publications, a division of Kregel, Inc., PO Box 2607, Grand Rapids, MI 49501.

Library of Congress Cataloging-in-Publication Data
Duvall, J. Scott.
Experiencing God's story of life and hope : a workbook for
    spiritual formation / by J. Scott Duvall.
    p. cm.
Includes bibliographical references (pp. 195–97) and index.
1. Spiritual formation—Textbooks. I. Title.
BV4511.D88   2008   248.4—dc22   2008036365

ISBN 978-0-8254-2538-7

Printed in the United States of America

09 10 11 12 / 5 4 3

CONTENTS

I would like to thank the following people for their help in developing this resource: Brandon O'Brien, Josh and Jill McCarty, Michael and Terese Cox, Julie (Byrum) Stone, Kristine (Lewis) Smith, and Brandon Holiski. The other pastoral leaders at Fellowship Church—Scott Jackson, Neal Nelson, and Darrell Bridges—have been very encouraging throughout the process. My daughter Meagan spent hours sitting in my office punching holes in each page and compiling the first round of books. Thanks, everyone!

Read Me First

Whether you were raised in the church and accepted Christ as your personal savior at age five, or whether you have only recently given your life to Christ, spiritual growth is not optional. God expects his children to *grow up!*

We define *spiritual formation* as the process of allowing God to conform us to the image of Jesus Christ. The Bible clearly teaches that God wants his children to grow to maturity. As you read the sampling of verses below, especially notice the italicized words.

> For those God foreknew he also predestined to be *conformed to the likeness of his Son*, that he might be the firstborn among many brothers. (Rom. 8:29)

> Therefore, I urge you, brothers, in view of God's mercy, to offer your bodies as living sacrifices, holy and pleasing to God—this is your spiritual act of worship. Do not conform any longer to the pattern of this world, but *be transformed* by the renewing of your mind. Then you will be able to test and approve what God's will is—his good, pleasing and perfect will. (Rom. 12:1–2)

> And we, who with unveiled faces all reflect the Lord's glory, are *being transformed into his likeness* with ever-increasing glory, which comes from the Lord, who is the Spirit. (2 Cor. 3:18)

> Therefore we do not lose heart. Though outwardly we are wasting away, yet inwardly *we are being renewed* day by day. (2 Cor. 4:16)

> My dear children, for whom I am again in the pains of childbirth *until Christ is formed in you* . . . (Gal. 4:19)

> You were taught, with regard to your former way of life, to put off your old self, which is being corrupted by its deceitful desires; to *be made new* in the attitude of your minds; and to put on the new self, *created to be like God* in true righteousness and holiness. (Eph. 4:22–24)

. . . being confident of this, that *he who began a good work in you will carry it on to completion* until the day of Christ Jesus. (Phil. 1:6)

Therefore, my dear friends, as you have always obeyed—not only in my presence, but now much more in my absence—continue to *work out your salvation* with fear and trembling, *for it is God who works in you* to will and to act according to his good purpose. (Phil. 2:12–13)

Have nothing to do with godless myths and old wives' tales; rather, *train yourself to be godly.* (1 Tim. 4:7)

Like newborn babies, crave pure spiritual milk, so that by it *you may grow up in your salvation*, now that you have tasted that the Lord is good. (1 Peter 2:2–3)

Each aspect of our definition of *spiritual formation* is significant. Spiritual formation is a *process*. We don't experience growth as a neat, clean, upward slope toward heaven. In reality it looks and feels more like a roller-coaster ride, twisting and turning and looping and climbing and dropping. Only as you stand back and see the big picture can you tell that the "exit" to the ride is higher than the "entrance." Spiritual formation is a messy process. Because we don't always cooperate with the Lord, it takes time for him to accomplish his purpose in our lives. Philippians 1:6 offers a great deal of encouragement here (see above). God never stops working.

Spiritual formation is the process of *allowing* God to work in our lives. God is sovereign but he has also created us to make important decisions and to bear the responsibility for those decisions. We have no power in and of ourselves to cause our own growth, nor will God force us to obey him. We must allow God to work in our lives and to bring about change. God deeply desires to work, but we must give him the necessary time and space. We don't cause our own growth, but we do cooperate with God as he works. Check out Philippians 2:12–13 above.

Spiritual formation is a process of allowing *God* to work in our lives. We are told that the Holy Spirit continues the earthly ministry that Jesus began (Acts 1:1–2). God's Spirit lives within each genuine believer (1 Cor. 6:19). Our growth is not the result of special circumstances or good luck. We don't grow by our own willpower or by striving to obey the Law. We grow when we follow the Holy Spirit, who alone can produce spiritual fruit in our lives (see Gal. 5:16–23). For us to be loving, joyful, peaceful, and so on, the Holy Spirit must be allowed to do his work.

Spiritual formation is the process of allowing God *to conform us* to the image of Jesus. As much as I hate to admit it, growth means change. Like clay in the potter's hand, we are shaped and molded and conformed to a particular pattern. Change at the hand of God is sometimes painful, but it is always good. We don't always like it, but deep down we always desire it because we know it is necessary. James tells us to "consider it pure joy . . . whenever you face trials of many kinds, because you know that the testing of your faith develops perseverance" and "perseverance must finish its work so that you may be mature and complete, not lacking anything" (James 1:2–4). God loves us too much to let us stay as we are.

Finally, spiritual formation is the process of allowing God to conform us *to the image of Jesus Christ*. In Romans 8:29; 2 Corinthians 3:18; and Galatians 4:19 (see page 9), we are told that God is making us more and more like his Son. Jesus is the perfect pattern or model. He represents the goal of spiritual formation. We are not being shaped into merely religious people or ethical people or church-going people. We are being conformed to the very character of Christ himself.

Everyone, without exception, experiences some kind of "spiritual formation." Dallas Willard puts it this way:

> All people undergo a process of spiritual formation. Their spirit is formed, and with it their whole being. . . . Spiritual formation is not something just for especially religious people. No one escapes. The most hardened criminal as well as the most devout of human beings have had a spiritual formation. They have become a certain kind of person. You have had a spiritual formation and I have had one, and it is still ongoing. It is like education: everyone gets one—a good one or a bad one. (*Renovation of the Heart*, 45)

Everyone is being formed by certain powers after a particular pattern or model. We are blessed beyond words to be able to participate in God's design for spiritual formation.

God often uses resources to shape or mold us into conformity with Christ's character. Of course, the primary resource is God's Word, the Bible. But there are also many good and helpful supplementary resources. We certainly know that no ministry resource of any kind can ever substitute for a personal relationship with God through Jesus Christ, but God does seem to use spiritual-growth resources to help our love for him grow deeper and stronger. *Experiencing God's Story of Life and Hope* is one particularly effective resource that God can use to help us understand and participate consistently in true, godly spiritual formation.

Believing-Behaving-Becoming

Most resources focus on just one aspect of the spiritual formation process. Some tools emphasize our *beliefs* by explaining the core teachings of the Christian faith. Knowing what to believe is crucial, but there is more. Many spiritual formation resources highlight how we should *behave*. They stress the importance of spiritual disciplines such as prayer, Bible study, solitude, worship, and so on. Without a doubt God uses such disciplines to transform our lives, but the disciplines are means to an end, not the end themselves.

The disciplines are like workout routines pointing toward the game itself. The game is our life with God. Finally, there are a handful of resources that pay attention to what people are *becoming* in the entire process of spiritual formation (i.e., godly character). Most of these center on the fruit of the Spirit as the true test of spirituality, and rightly so.

Experiencing God's Story of Life and Hope connects all three aspects of spiritual formation: what we believe, how we behave, and who we are becoming. All three are essential to our growth:

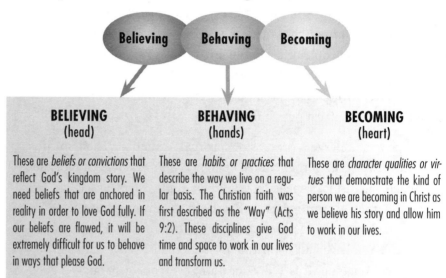

BELIEVING (head)	BEHAVING (hands)	BECOMING (heart)
These are *beliefs or convictions* that reflect God's kingdom story. We need beliefs that are anchored in reality in order to love God fully. If our beliefs are flawed, it will be extremely difficult for us to behave in ways that please God.	These are *habits or practices* that describe the way we live on a regular basis. The Christian faith was first described as the "Way" (Acts 9:2). These disciplines give God time and space to work in our lives and transform us.	These are *character qualities or virtues* that demonstrate the kind of person we are becoming in Christ as we believe his story and allow him to work in our lives.

As a teaching tool, this workbook connects a "Believing" area with a "Behaving" area and a "Becoming" area. Look at the overview on pages 16–17 to see the whole plan. For example, in the third row of the overview you will notice a belief in a great and good God. That belief is connected to the habit of worship and to the quality of purity or holiness. In other words, each row of the overview is connected and integrated; each belief is tied to a behavior or habit and then to a character quality.

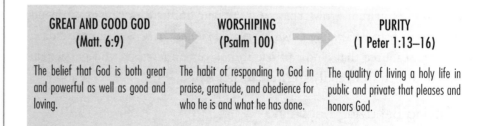

GREAT AND GOOD GOD (Matt. 6:9)	WORSHIPING (Psalm 100)	PURITY (1 Peter 1:13–16)
The belief that God is both great and powerful as well as good and loving.	The habit of responding to God in praise, gratitude, and obedience for who he is and what he has done.	The quality of living a holy life in public and private that pleases and honors God.

This Believing-Behaving-Becoming arrangement is merely a teaching tool and is not intended as a rigid religious system. Sometimes beliefs lead to behavior, while at other times behavior influences beliefs. I'm not suggesting a 1-2-3, neat, clean, foolproof, linear progression that will solve all of life's problems. We all know that life is messy, dynamic, unpredictable, confusing, spontaneous, mystical, and so on. But I still think there are important connections to be made using this teaching arrangement. For instance, what we believe about Satan and sin will affect how we fight spiritual battles and how we understand and experience true freedom. While recognizing this somewhat artificial organization, I hope the Believing-Behaving-Becoming setup encourages you to allow the Lord to work in your entire life rather than just one area of your life.

The overview includes a total of thirty-six boxes of beliefs, behaviors, and character qualities.

Why these particular topics? Were they chosen simply because they are the most popular topics when it comes to spiritual growth? Are we looking at a random bunch of beliefs and habits and virtues all loosely connected? Actually, the topics were not chosen at random or through some popularity contest. These topics reflect God's story and in our context today we definitely need to stay anchored to God's story.

Experiencing God's Story of Life and Hope

Since the late 1960s we have been experiencing a cultural shift from modernism to postmodernism. (See Jimmy Long's excellent book *Emerging Hope* for more on this cultural change and how Christians can respond.) The modern era emphasized the individual, objective truth, words, and some kind of grand story to explain the meaning of life. By contrast, the postmodern era emphasizes community, subjective "truth," images, and the absence of any grand story to explain life. Christians can embrace some aspects of postmodernism and probably need to resist others. For instance, we can certainly celebrate the greater emphasis on community. But if we give up on a big story that explains reality, then we might as well give up on our faith.

The Christian faith is founded upon God's grand story revealed in the Bible. Postmodernism does away with all big stories that claim to explain reality, opting instead for local or small-group stories. What is true for me and my friends is what is true—period! But Christians can't abandon God's grand story or there is nothing left to believe and all hope is lost. Instead, we need to understand God's story even more and see how it connects to life and how it does us good. We would say that what is real and true is not just what my local group prefers, but what God has revealed. God's story explains life.

Spiritual formation needs to be connected to God's story or it can be manipulated to mean almost anything. In other words, we need a biblical story approach to spiritual formation. But we obviously need to do more than just "believe" the story. We need to act upon the story and allow God's story to shape our whole being. Perhaps now the title makes more sense. We need to experience (beliefs, habits, character qualities) God's story (as revealed in the Bible) of life and hope (a story that does what is best for us).

How is this story approach built into this workbook? It's simple. If you look again at the overview you will notice that the "Believing" column is actually God's grand story.

BELIEVING	(meaning in the story)
Authority of the Bible	A trustworthy script for the story
Triune God who is Great and Good	Begins with God who is community
Humanity	God wants to share his community
Satan and Sin	Evil powers try to ruin the plan
Jesus Christ	The hero of the story
Salvation	The rescue begins
Holy Spirit	God with us until the end
The Church	The community being rescued
Transformation	God works among his children
Mission	God works through his children
The End	The end—we are with God in the new creation

The very first item in the column is the *Bible* or the script of the story. The story proper begins with *God*—who he is and what he has done. God creates *human beings* to relate to him in perfect community, but *Satan and sin* spoil God's good creation and interfere with his story. God must now attempt a rescue to save his creation. Because of his great love for us, God sent his Son *Jesus Christ* to rescue us from Satan and sin and restore us to a relationship with him. *Salvation* means that God has come to rescue us from the dark side. Through Christ, God offers us a way home. As we respond to his gracious offer by trusting him, we are adopted by God into his family. He puts his very own *Spirit* within us and incorporates us into his community. God desires to use this *new community* (called *church*) to provide us with identity, stability, and wholeness. As we eat, pray, worship, and listen to God's Word together, we begin to feel safe. We open up, revealing our joys and struggles. We discover that we can really be known and loved at the same time, rather than just one or the other. Perhaps for the first time we experience life and hope through Christ and his community. We are *transformed* into the kind of person we were created to be. Naturally, we want other people to experience this life and hope. We have a *mission*—to live out God's story in biblical community so that others can join God's community. Since it is a story of hope, God's story *ends* happily (read Rev. 21:1–4).

INTRODUCTION

To summarize, the "Believing" column is God's grand story. Spiritual formation is anchored in God's story. As we move through the story (from top to bottom), each Belief area extends out (from left to right) to a Behaving and a Becoming area. In this way our whole life is being shaped by the Lord and the entire process is firmly secured to God's story.

Workbook Format

Most of the studies in the workbook consist of the following elements:

- An introduction that explores the biblical context
- "A Closer Look," to dig deeper into a particular text
- "Crossing the Bridge," to move from the ancient world to our world
- "So What?" to apply what we have discovered in the context of biblical community
- "The Power of Words," to help you understand the meaning of words in the text
- Insightful quotes that inspire reflection and action
- Application questions for your small group
- Cross-references for more Bible exploration
- A "For Deeper Study" recommended reading list

In terms of assumptions, characteristics, and benefits, *Experiencing God's Story of Life and Hope* is:

- theologically grounded in the evangelical Christian tradition
- spiritually integrated by connecting believing, behaving, and becoming
- academically reliable through the use of solid biblical scholarship
- pedagogically interactive without being insulting (i.e., you won't find rhetorical fill-in-the-blank questions)
- creatively designed to be used by individuals within the context of biblical community
- practically and realistically arranged into 12 three-part chapters

Another subtle characteristic worth mentioning is that the workbook teaches by example how to do responsible Bible study. The move from context to observation to theological principle to application follows the journey model detailed in *Grasping God's Word* by Scott Duvall and Daniel Hays. Thirty-six weeks of handling the Scriptures responsibly will have a positive impact on students of the Bible.

May the Lord bless you richly as you allow him to conform you to the image of Jesus Christ. I pray that *Experiencing God's Story of Life and Hope* will serve you well on your journey.

Overview

BELIEVING	BEHAVING	BECOMING
Authority of the Bible (2 Tim. 3:16–17)	**Studying the Bible** (2 Tim. 2:15)	**Truth** (Eph. 4:20–25)
The belief that the Bible is God's inspired Word given to us to help us mature in our faith.	The habit of reading, interpreting, and applying the Bible as the primary means of listening to God.	The quality of living and speaking truthfully in a world of lies and deception.
Triune God (Gal. 4:4–6)	**Fellowshiping** (Acts 2:42–47)	**Love** (1 John 4:7–8)
The belief that the Bible teaches the triune (three-in-one) nature of God.	The habit of living in authentic relationship with and dependence upon other followers of Jesus.	The quality of choosing to do what God says is best for another person.
Great and Good God (Matt. 6:9)	**Worshiping** (Psalm 100)	**Purity** (1 Peter 1:13–16)
The belief that God is both great and powerful as well as good and loving.	The habit of responding to God in praise, gratitude, and obedience for who he is and what he has done.	The quality of living a holy life in public and private that pleases and honors God.
Humanity (Gen. 1:26–28)	**Seeking the Kingdom** (Matt. 6:33)	**Rest** (Matt. 11:28–30)
The belief that human beings are uniquely created in the image of God.	The habit of acknowledging that God is our Creator and that we are creatures intended to seek him and his purposes.	The quality of living with a deep awareness of and contentment with God's purpose for our lives.
Satan and Sin (Gen. 3:1–7)	**Waging Spiritual War** (Matt. 4:1–11)	**Freedom** (Rom. 8:1–4)
The belief that Satan is the leader of the opposition against God and his people, and that all human beings have a willful opposition to God's claim on their lives (sin).	The habit of knowing and using appropriate strategies for fighting against the Devil, the flesh, and the world.	The quality of experiencing freedom from Satan's power and sin's domination and freedom for new life with God.
Jesus Christ (John 1:1–3, 14, 18)	**Following** (Mark 8:34–38)	**New Identity in Christ** (John 21:15–23)
The belief that Jesus Christ is God the Son, fully divine and fully human.	The habit of daily choosing to follow Jesus Christ as Lord in every area of life.	The quality of single-minded allegiance to Jesus Christ above every other competing loyalty.

BELIEVING	BEHAVING	BECOMING
Salvation (Eph. 2:8–10) The belief that salvation is by grace (source), through faith (means), for good works (result).	**Trusting and Acting** (Phil. 2:12–13) The habit of allowing God to work in our lives so that our faith results in action (not salvation by works, but true faith that works).	**Assurance** (Rom. 8:15–16) The quality of knowing (with a healthy confidence) that we belong to God.
Holy Spirit (John 14:16–17) The belief that God the Spirit continues Jesus' earthly ministry, especially that of transforming believers and empowering them to fulfill their mission.	**Walking by the Spirit** (Gal. 5:16, 25) The habit of living in dependence upon the Holy Spirit as the source of strength to resist temptation and imitate Jesus Christ.	**Fruit of the Spirit** (Gal. 5:22–24) The quality of bearing the fruit of the Holy Spirit (Christlike character qualities) in one's life.
The Church (1 Peter 2:4–10) The belief that God's people are joined together in Christ into a new community, the church.	**Serving** (Mark 10:35–45) The habit of being a servant to other members of this new community.	**Humility** (Luke 18:9–14) The quality of a servant's attitude grounded in the recognition of our status before God and our relationship to others.
Transformation (Rom. 12:1–2) The belief that we are not to be conformed to this world, but we are to be transformed into the image of Jesus Christ.	**Praying** (Matt. 6:9–13) The habit of continual communion with God that fosters our relationship and allows for genuine transformation in our lives.	**Peace** (Phil. 4:6–7) The quality of calmness and well being (vs. worry and inner turmoil) that comes as a result of our communion with God.
Mission (Matt. 28:18–20) The belief that Jesus commissioned his church to make disciples of all nations.	**Engaging the World** (Acts 1:7–8) The habit of engaging the world for the purpose of sharing the good news of Jesus Christ.	**Compassion** (Luke 10:30–37) The quality of extending love and compassion to people in need.
The End (1 Thess. 4:13–18) The belief that Jesus Christ will return to judge evil, restore his creation, and live forever in intimate fellowship with his people.	**Persevering** (Heb. 12:1–2) The habit of enduring and persisting in spite of the trials and difficulties we face in life.	**Hope** (Rom. 8:22–25) The quality of a confident expectation that in the end God will be true to his word and keep his promises.

God Talk

Authority of the Bible

I've never been scuba diving, but I'm told that it's a blast. Strapping on those life tanks and exploring the water world below sounds like fun. Of course it's not all fun and games. A former Navy diver once told me that he had been in waters so deep and dark that it was almost impossible to keep from becoming disoriented and confused. What a terrifying feeling it must be—being under water, unable to see your hands in front of your face, not knowing which way is up, panic engulfing you. I immediately interrupted my friend. "So what did you do?" I knew he had survived the ordeal since he was standing there talking to me. "Feel the bubbles," he said. "When it's pitch black and you have no idea which way to go, you reach up with your hand and feel the bubbles. The bubbles always drift to the surface. When you can't trust your feelings or judgment, you can always trust the bubbles to get you back to the top."

I have no intention of ever diving that deep and getting myself into that situation, but it's nice to know that I could always "feel the bubbles" as a reality check. Life is like scuba diving in that we need a way to determine what is real and true. Sometimes in life we get disoriented and desperate. At other times, we find ourselves drifting aimlessly. God knew that we would need instructions and examples about how to live. In the sixty-six books of the Bible, we have a reality library—stories, letters, guidelines, and examples from God that tell us what is true and real. In a world that is changing faster than we can imagine, we have something stable, true, and real. The Bible is our reality book, an amazing gift from God, who loves us deeply and desires a relationship with us.

A Closer Look—2 Timothy 3:16–17

God is the divine author of the Bible, choosing to work through many human authors over a period of time to give us his message. We use the word *inspiration* to describe God's work as the divine source of the Bible. The apostle Paul speaks of the divine inspiration of Scripture in 2 Timothy 3:16–17:

> ¹⁶All Scripture is God-breathed [inspired] and is useful for teaching, rebuking, correcting and training in righteousness, ¹⁷so that the man of God may be thoroughly equipped for every good work.

What Was Jesus' View of Scripture?
Do not think that I have come to abolish the Law or the Prophets; I have not come to abolish them but to fulfill them. I tell you the truth, until heaven and earth disappear, not the smallest letter, not the least stroke of a pen, will by any means disappear from the Law until everything is accomplished.
—Matthew 5:17–18

In 2 Timothy 3:16–17 the term "Scripture" refers specifically to the Old Testament. What does it refer to in 1 Timothy 5:18? How about 2 Peter 3:16?

Let's take a closer look at this text to get a better idea of what the Bible is and why God gave it to us.

Looking closely at a passage of Scripture is a lot like listening to another person—it takes time, concentration, and effort. The first step in listening to God's Word is understanding the passage's context, that is, the surrounding words, sentences, and paragraphs. Look up 2 Timothy in your Bible, and read the paragraph before and the paragraph after 3:16–17.

1. Who is writing this book, and to whom is he writing? (See 2 Tim. 1:1–2.)

2. In 3:10–13 Paul contrasts his way of life with the lifestyle of what group (see 3:1–9)?

3. What is Paul's specific command to Timothy in 3:14? What are the two reasons why Timothy should be motivated to continue in what he has learned (see 3:14–15)?

4. In 3:16 what are the two things that "Scripture is"?

Inspired by God

Paul says that Scripture is "God-breathed." What does this expression mean? Some versions translate the Greek word as "inspired," but the NIV has chosen "God-breathed"—a good translation. This is much more than saying that the Bible is inspiring, like a good movie or a romantic sunset. To say that the Bible is God-breathed, or inspired, is to say that it is God's Word. All Scripture, not just some of it, comes from the mouth of God. To read the Bible is to hear God speak, and what God speaks is completely true and reliable. What Scripture says, God says.

We are told that Scripture is both "God-breathed," or inspired, and useful or helpful. The order is important. Scripture is profitable and beneficial to us in life and ministry *because* it comes from God.

Profitable for Us

In the last part of verse 16 we are told that Scripture is useful or profitable for four things. What are those four things, and how do they relate to each other?

So Scripture comes from God and therefore proves helpful to us. But helpful in what sense? In 3:17 we find that the purpose of Scripture is accomplished in our lives when we read it and take it to heart. What is that purpose?

Summary

Let's say that you want to be a person of God who is "thoroughly equipped for every good work" (v. 17b). Summarize the advice given in 3:16–17 about how to become so equipped.

Jesus Believed the Bible

The first and foremost reason why Christians believe in the divine inspiration and authority of Scripture is . . . because of what Jesus Christ himself said. Since he endorsed the authority of Scripture, we are bound to conclude that his authority and Scripture's authority either stand or fall together. . . . All the available evidence confirms that Jesus Christ assented in his mind and submitted in his life to the authority of Old Testament Scripture. Is it not inconceivable that his followers should have a lower view of it than he?

—John Stott,
Authentic Christianity, 96

THE POWER OF WORDS

"teaching"—This word, frequently translated "doctrine," shows up often in Paul's letters to Timothy and Titus (1 Tim. 1:10; 4:1, 6, 13, 16; 5:17; 6:1, 3; 2 Tim. 3:16; 4:3; Titus 1:9; 2:1, 7, 10) and refers to reliable instruction in Christian belief and conduct. Scripture plays a primary role in equipping Christians in belief and behavior.

"rebuking"—This word refers to pointing out as well as refuting erroneous beliefs and practices.

"correcting"—This is the positive side to rebuking and deals with how to set everything right once the error has been identified. Scripture helps us restore or change our beliefs and practices.

"training in righteousness"—This phrase speaks of Scripture's role in helping us stay on the proper path through teaching and instruction in God's ways.

In 2 Timothy 3:14–4:2 Paul refers to the Scriptures in four ways. What are they?

?

The Primacy of Scripture

A writer and teacher who chose and ordered his words carefully, Mr. Lewis put "Scripture, the Church, Christian friends, books, etc." in this order by design. To him these avenues of revelation were not equal. Scripture, to Lewis, is the place where we hear God most clearly and definitively. Scripture is the litmus test of the validity of all other sources of Divine guidance. When the church, a book, or a Christian friend instructs in a way contradictory to the plenary meaning of the Bible, C. S. Lewis firmly dismissed the other voices.

—Lyle Dorsett,
Seeking the Secret Place, 52

Cross-References
Ps. 119; John 17:17; Rom. 15:4; Heb. 4:12; 2 Peter 1:20–21

For Deeper Study
Dockery, David S. *Christian Scripture.* Nashville: Broadman & Holman, 1995.

Marshall, I. Howard. *Biblical Inspiration.* Grand Rapids: Eerdmans, 1982.

Stott, John R. W. *Evangelical Truth: A Personal Plea for Unity, Integrity and Faithfulness.* Downers Grove, IL: InterVarsity Press, 1999.

So What?

1. Some people don't respect the Bible and deny its authority altogether. What other authority or authorities do they put in place of the Scriptures?

2. Sometimes those of us who hold to the authority of the Bible struggle to live out that belief in a consistent way. Would your friends and family say that your life demonstrates your belief in the authority of Scripture? What causes us to struggle to allow God's Word to have its rightful place of authority in our lives?

3. What is the best advice you have ever received about how to connect more consistently with God's Word?

4. What can you do this week to be more faithful to listening to God through his Word?

Handle with Care

Studying the Bible

If we really believe in the authority of the Bible, we will want to read it and study it on a regular basis. Some Christians, however, don't study the Word because they don't know how. They think the Bible is just for professionals or they feel intimidated or embarrassed by what they don't know. What you will learn in Behaving 1 will help you gain confidence in your ability to understand what God is saying to you through his Word. The experience of learning how to study the Scriptures will cultivate in you a firsthand faith, resulting in greater joy and excitement about following Jesus.

Studying the Bible is like taking a journey. Every time you open your Bible and read a passage, you are reading about people who lived and events that happened a long time ago. Yet because neither God's character nor human nature change, God's Word remains timeless and forever relevant. Don't worry, we don't bear the burden of having to make the Bible relevant; it is already relevant. We do, however, need to discover and explore how it relates to our lives. We need a reliable way to understand God's Word as it was intended. That's where the image of a journey proves helpful. (The journey image is taken from Scott Duvall and Daniel Hays, *Grasping God's Word*.) The "journey of the Bible" includes four steps:

1. *The meaning for the Biblical audience.* What did the passage mean to the biblical audience, to the people who first heard the words that we are now reading?
2. *The river of differences.* What are the differences and similarities between the biblical audience and us?

36 Life Essentials

BELIEVING
Authority of the Bible
Triune God
Great and Good God
Humanity
Satan and Sin
Jesus Christ
Salvation
Holy Spirit
The Church
Transformation
Mission
The End

BEHAVING
➤ **Studying the Bible**
Fellowshiping
Worshiping
Seeking the Kingdom
Waging Spiritual War
Following
Trusting and Acting
Walking by the Spirit
Serving
Praying
Engaging the World
Persevering

BECOMING
Truth
Love
Purity
Rest
Freedom
New Identity in Christ
Assurance
Fruit of the Spirit
Humility
Peace
Compassion
Hope

In your opinion, what are the top five reasons why people do not study the Bible?

1.

2.

3.

4.

5.

Knowing Firsthand

The ultimate benefit of firsthand Bible study is that you will fall in love with the Author. You see, it's hard to fall in love by proxy. Sermons, books, commentaries, and so on—those can be wonderful resources to spiritual growth. But they are all secondhand. If you want to know God directly, you need to encounter His Word directly.

—Howard Hendricks and William Hendricks, *Living By the Book*, 33

3. *The bridge of theological principles.* What are the timeless theological principles in the text that connect with both the biblical audience and with us?
4. *Contemporary application.* How can we apply that meaning to our lives today?

We begin our journey in the ancient world because that is where God first spoke his Word. If we ignore the ancient meaning, we will be tempted to make the Bible say what we want it to say, rather than discovering what it really says and means. We don't stay in the ancient world, since that wouldn't do us any good. Instead we cross into our world using a bridge built upon timeless, theological principles. Only then can we apply the meaning of the text to our lives. Let's look at each phase of the journey using 2 Timothy 2:15 as our example text. Open your Bible to 2 Timothy 2, and begin your journey.

1. The Meaning for the Biblical Audience

To grasp what the text meant to the biblical audience, you first need to understand the context. Read the verses before your passage as well as the verses that follow. What do you see in the surrounding context that helps you understand what Paul meant in verse 15?

We also need to find out about the historical situation that caused Paul to write to Timothy in the first place. A good study Bible (e.g., *The NIV Study Bible*) will tell you about the historical context of a book. Look in your study Bible at the beginning of both 1 and 2 Timothy and read about the author, setting, purpose, reasons for writing, and things like these. Is there anything in this information that helps you understand what Paul meant in 2:15?

After you get a feel for the context, look carefully at the passage itself. Circle important words, underline commands, bracket figures of speech, identify contrasts and comparisons, notice how significant nouns are described, be aware of the tone of the passage, and so on. Mark up the passage below with your observations. Don't worry about what it all means at this point, just look carefully at what it says.

Do your best to present yourself to God

as one approved, a workman

who does not need to be ashamed

and who correctly handles the word of truth.

Can you summarize what Paul meant when he wrote 2 Timothy 2:15?

What are the main traits of the false teaching that Timothy is fighting in Ephesus (see 2 Tim. 2:16–3:9)?

2. The River of Differences

Sometimes the river separating us from the biblical audience is narrow and shallow (e.g., James 1:19: "Everyone should be quick to listen, slow to speak and slow to become angry"). At other times, however, the river is wide and deep (e.g., 1 Cor. 11:4: "Every man who prays or prophesies with his head covered dishonors his head"). How does our situation differ from the circumstances Paul and Timothy faced?

How is our situation similar to theirs?

THE POWER OF WORDS

"correctly handles"—A metaphor that literally means "to cut straight." The background of the metaphor is unclear. It could refer to a stone mason making a straight cut, or to a farmer cutting a straight furrow, or to a person walking in a straight line. In any case, Paul is telling Timothy to handle the Christian message accurately, unlike the false teachers.

3. The Bridge of Theological Principles

We cross the bridge from the ancient world to our world by identifying theological truths that God intended to communicate through Paul to Timothy and the Ephesian church, and ultimately to us. This is the most challenging part of Bible study but also the most crucial for "handling the Word correctly." Write out a present-tense statement or principle that captures the heart of 2:15 by completing the following statement:

All Christians, but especially those church leaders responsible for the ministry of the Word, are supposed to . . .

This is your *theological principle*. Ask yourself the following questions to test the validity of the principle you have identified.

- Does your statement reflect what the Bible actually says and means?
- Is your statement relevant to both the ancient situation and the contemporary situation? A theological principle will be timeless and apply equally to both audiences.
- Is your statement consistent with the teaching of the rest of the Bible?

4. Contemporary Application

When you cross the bridge of theological principles, you are identifying the meaning of the text. We do not determine the meaning; we discover the meaning and then respond to that meaning. We refer to this response as "application." While the meaning of a passage never changes and is the same for all Christians, the application of that meaning may be different for every Christian. As you think about the context and meaning of 2 Timothy 2:15, what specific application is the Holy Spirit leading you to make part of your life? In other words, what particular changes does God want to make in your life related to how you handle the Bible?

So What?

1. Do you see a difference between reading the Bible and studying the Bible? Explain.

2. Are you really convinced deep down that you need to study the Bible? Why or why not?

3. What will happen over the long run if a person neglects (for whatever reason) the study of the Scriptures? What is your greatest struggle when it comes to Bible study?

4. Knowing that life change occurs in small increments ("little by little"), what one, small, realistic thing could you do this week to study God's Word more faithfully?

Cross-References
Ps. 119; Matt. 4:4; Acts 6:4; Col. 3:16; 1 Peter 2:1–2

For Deeper Study
Duvall, J. Scott, and J. Daniel Hays. *Grasping God's Word: A Hands-On Approach to Reading, Interpreting, and Applying the Bible.* 2nd ed. Grand Rapids: Zondervan, 2005.

Duvall, J. Scott, and J. Daniel Hays. *Journey into God's Word: Your Guide to Understanding and Applying the Bible.* Grand Rapids: Zondervan, 2007.

Fee, Gordon D., and Douglas Stuart. *How to Read the Bible for All Its Worth.* 3rd ed. Grand Rapids: Zondervan, 2003.

Hendricks, Howard G., and William D. Hendricks. *Living By the Book.* Revised and expanded. Chicago: Moody, 2007.

The Whole Truth and Nothing but the Truth

Truth

As what we believe and how we behave come together, they shape who we become. One quality that results from believing and studying the Bible is the quality of a truthful life. In our world truth is often considered an inconvenient liability rather than a godly asset, yet we know that God himself is the author of truth. If we want a meaningful relationship with the Lord, commitment to truth is not an option but a life essential. In fact, Jesus said, "I am the way and the truth and the life" (John 14:6). God is truth, and the closer we walk with him, the more truthful our lives will be. In Becoming 1 we will explore how we can live and speak truthfully in an age of exaggeration, spin, lies, and deceit.

We do indeed live in an age of spin. Bill Press, former host of CNN's *Crossfire*, attempts a definition:

There is no good definition of spin. It's easier to say what it's not than what it is: It's not the truth. Neither is it a lie. Spin lies somewhere in between: almost telling the truth, but not quite; bending the truth to make things look as good—or as bad—as possible; painting things in the best possible—or worst possible—light. (*Spin This*, xiv)

The first-century Roman world also had its share of spin doctors. The apostle Paul and other Christian teachers and missionaries had to distinguish themselves from popular preachers called Sophists who traveled around using their slick image and polished speaking ability to impress the crowds and pad their bank accounts. These swindlers would gladly twist the truth for personal profit. Paul does not hesitate to tell the churches that he and his coworkers would have nothing to do with such underhanded methods of spreading the gospel.

Unlike so many, we do not peddle the word of God for profit. On the contrary, in Christ we speak before God with sincerity, like men sent from God. . . . Rather, we have renounced secret and shameful ways; we do not use deception, nor do we distort the word of God. On the contrary, by setting forth the truth plainly we commend ourselves to every man's conscience in the sight of God. (2 Cor. 2:17; 4:2)

For the appeal we make does not spring from error or impure motives, nor are we trying to trick you. . . . You know we never used flattery, nor did we put on a mask to cover up greed—God is our witness. We were not looking for praise from men, not from you or anyone else. (1 Thess. 2:3, 5–6)

Clearly, truth twisting has always been a temptation for people living in a world where sin abounds. How, then, are Christians to live truthfully in a culture where falsehood is the norm?

A Closer Look—Ephesians 4:20–25

We see in Ephesians 4:20–25 a summary of Paul's advice on speaking and living truthfully.

Wearing a Mask?

When people fail to live the truth they speak, we call them hypocrites. A hypocrite says one thing and does another. Our word *hypocrite* comes from the ancient Greek word *hypokritēs*. Classically, it denoted the actor in a drama who played a role on stage, often wearing a mask as part of a costume. In time *hypokritēs* came to have the negative connotation we associate with the English word *hypocrite*.

—Mark Roberts,
Dare to Be True, 143

SCRIPTURE NOTES

[20]You, however, did not come to know Christ that way. [21]Surely you heard of him and were taught in him in accordance with the truth that is in Jesus. [22]You were taught, with regard to your former way of life, to put off your old self, which is being corrupted by its deceitful desires; [23]to be made new in the attitude of your minds; [24]and to put on the new self, created to be like God in true righteousness and holiness. [25]Therefore each of you must put off falsehood and speak truthfully to his neighbor, for we are all members of one body.

The Old Testament has a lot to say about truth, often connecting it closely with faithfulness—a quality that fosters trust and makes relationships thrive. What do the following texts from Psalms teach us about truth?

• 15:1–2

• 40:11

• 43:3

• 51:6

• 86:11, 15

• 119:160

• 138:2

• 145:18

"falsehood"—The Greek word *pseudos* refers to a false statement or a lie, spoken with the intent to mislead or deceive. While God is the author of truth, Satan is the father of lies (John 8:44). Those who follow Jesus Christ are committed to truth (Rev. 14:5; 21:27), whereas those who are opposed to Christ prefer lies and deception (Rom. 1:25; 1 Tim. 4:1–2; Rev. 22:15).

1. To understand a text and apply its meaning to our lives, we always start with context. Read Ephesians 4:14–32 and note anything that helps you understand what Paul meant by the commands to "put off falsehood and speak truthfully" found in verse 25.

2. The word *however* in 4:20 indicates a contrast. What stands in contrast to the way the Ephesians came to know Christ? (What you win them with, you win them to!)

3. What is the basis or foundation of the command in 4:25 (see 4:21–24)? How does our identity in Christ relate to our experience of living truthfully?

4. Identify the negative command, the positive command, and the reason for the commands that Paul presents in 4:25. How do the two commands relate? Can you obey one without obeying the other?

Crossing the Bridge

Write a present-tense statement that captures the theological heart of Ephesians 4:25. Often in New Testament letters, the "river" separating us from the biblical audience is neither wide nor deep, so your statement may sound a lot like the verse.

As a way of validating the theological principle that you have just written, you can ask the following questions:

- Does your statement reflect what the text actually says and means?
- Is your statement relevant to both the ancient situation and the contemporary situation? A theological principle will be timeless and apply equally to both audiences.
- Is your statement consistent with the teaching of the rest of the Bible?

So What?

1. Have you ever been hurt by a lie (yours or someone else's)? Explain.

2. Why is lying a relationship killer?

3. Think about a recent situation where you were not completely honest. What pressured or motivated you to lie or spin the truth?

4. What helps you to recognize and to reject falsehood and deception?

Jesus said, "Simply let your 'Yes' be 'Yes,' and your 'No,' 'No'; anything beyond this comes from the evil one" (Matt. 5:37). What did he mean?

Growing Up

Then [as the church moves toward maturity] we will no longer be infants, tossed back and forth by the waves, and blown here and there by every wind of teaching and by the cunning and craftiness of men in their deceitful scheming. Instead, speaking the truth in love, we will in all things grow up into him who is the Head, that is, Christ.

—Ephesians 4:14–15

With reference to Eph. 4:15, which is the greater temptation for you, speaking (in love) something besides the truth or speaking the truth without love?

Cross-References
John 8:32; 14:6; 15:26; 16:13; 17:17; 2 Cor. 2:17; 4:2; Eph. 4:14–15; 6:14; Col. 3:9–10; 1 Thess. 2:3, 5–6; 1 John 2:21; 3:19–20; 5:20; 3 John 4

For Deeper Study
Baucham, Voddie. *The Ever-Loving Truth.* Nashville: Broadman & Holman, 2004.

Groothuis, Douglas. *Truth Decay.* Downers Grove, IL: InterVarsity Press, 2000.

Komp, Diane M. *Anatomy of a Lie: The Truth About Lies and Why Good People Tell Them.* Grand Rapids: Zondervan, 1998.

Lindsley, Art. *True Truth: Defending Absolute Truth in a Relativisitic World.* Downers Grove, IL: InterVarsity Press, 2004.

Matlock, Mark. *Don't Buy the Lie: Discerning Truth in a World of Deception.* Grand Rapids: Zondervan, 2004.

Roberts, Mark D. *Dare to Be True: Living in the Freedom of Complete Honesty.* Colorado Springs: Waterbrook, 2003.

5. Is there a person in your life who exemplifies truthful living? What would it take for you to be more like that person?

6. What specific steps can you take now to live more truthfully (e.g., Scripture memory, accountability partner, examining your motives)?

7. How can your Christian community promote truthfulness?

Three in One and One in Three

Triune God

For many people (some Christians included) the doctrine of the Trinity is about as exciting as doing advanced math blindfolded—overly complicated, boring, mysterious, and pointless. What difference does the obscure doctrine of God as Trinity really make after all? Why do we have to try to solve this theological puzzle? The simple answer is that this belief matters greatly if you want to know God and experience his salvation. Only God can save a person, and if God was not in Christ reconciling the world to himself (2 Cor. 5:19), then we cannot be in a right relationship with God. What sets Christianity apart from other religions is that we believe in one God who is Father, Son, and Spirit with each playing a unique role in rescuing lost humanity. In Believing 2, we will explore what it means to believe in the triune God revealed in Scripture. The relevance of this belief might surprise you.

The Oneness of God

The earliest Christians were Jews, and part of their Jewish heritage was a deeply held belief in the oneness of God (monotheism). The followers of the one God have always lived in a culture of multiple "gods"—the planets, the emperor, the inner self, wealth, or whatever. In sailing against the prevailing winds of polytheism (a belief in many gods), Christians followed the lead of their Master. For example, when asked about the greatest commandment, Jesus based his response on the oneness of God (Deut. 6:4–5).

> One of the teachers of the law came and heard them debating. Noticing that Jesus had given them a good answer, he asked him, "Of all the commandments, which is the most important?" "The most important one," answered Jesus, "is this: 'Hear, O Israel, the Lord our God, the Lord is one. Love the Lord your God with all your heart and with all your soul and with all your mind and with all your

strength.' The second is this: 'Love your neighbor as yourself.' There is no commandment greater than these." (Mark 12:28–31)

Along with this central passage from Deuteronomy, there are many other biblical texts that affirm that there is only one true God (e.g., Deut. 4:35, 39; 1 Kings 8:59–61; Isa. 43:10–11; Rom. 3:28–30; 1 Cor. 8:4, 6; 1 Tim. 1:17; 2:5; James 2:19).

The Deity of the Three

When we read the word *God* in the Bible, it normally refers to God the Father. Scripture clearly teaches that God the Father is divine. Based on the clear teaching of Scripture, Christians also believe that both Jesus Christ and the Holy Spirit are divine. Below you can read a few verses that teach the deity of both the Son and the Spirit.

> The high priest said to him, "I charge you under oath by the living God: Tell us if you are the Christ, the Son of God." "Yes, it is as you say," Jesus replied. (Matt. 26:63b–64a)

> In the beginning was the Word, and the Word was with God, and the Word was God. He was with God in the beginning. . . . The Word became flesh and made his dwelling among us. We have seen his glory, the glory of the One and Only, who came from the Father, full of grace and truth. (John 1:1–2, 14)

> [Jesus said,] "I and the Father are one." (John 10:30)

> Then Peter said, "Ananias, how is it that Satan has so filled your heart that you have lied to the Holy Spirit and have kept for yourself some of the money you received for the land? Didn't it belong to you before it was sold? And after it was sold, wasn't the money at your disposal? What made you think of doing such a thing? You have not lied to men but to God." (Acts 5:3–4)

> Don't you know that you yourselves are God's temple and that God's Spirit lives in you? If anyone destroys God's temple, God will destroy him; for God's temple is sacred, and you are that temple. (1 Cor. 3:16–17)

> Do you not know that your body is a temple of the Holy Spirit, who is in you, whom you have received from God? You are not your own; you were bought at a price. Therefore honor God with your body. (1 Cor. 6:19–20)

> In the past God spoke to our forefathers through the prophets at many times and in various ways, but in these last days he has spoken to us by his Son, whom he appointed heir of all things, and through whom he made the universe. The Son is the radiance of

God's glory and the exact representation of his being, sustaining all things by his powerful word. (Heb. 1:1–3a)

Triune God (Three-in-One)

The belief in God as Trinity comes from taking all of Scripture seriously. The Bible teaches God's oneness as well as the deity of Father, Son, and Spirit. There are not three separate Gods. There is only one God, but he always has and always will exist in three persons—Father, Son, and Spirit—all of whom are equally God. Thus, the "triune nature of God" refers to the one God in three persons.

There are a number of places in the Bible where the triune nature of God is captured in a verse or two. For example, Jesus teaches us to make disciples of all nations, "baptizing them in the name [singular] of the Father and of the Son and of the Holy Spirit" (Matt. 28:19). Speaking about the one God giving a variety of spiritual gifts, the apostle Paul says, "There are different kinds of gifts, but the same Spirit. There are different kinds of service, but the same Lord. There are different kinds of working, but the same God works all of them in all men" (1 Cor. 12:4–6). Paul also speaks of God's triune nature when encouraging the Corinthian Christians.

> Now it is *God* who makes both us and you stand firm in *Christ*. He anointed us, set his seal of ownership on us, and put his *Spirit* in our hearts as a deposit, guaranteeing what is to come. (2 Cor. 1:21–22)

> May the grace of the *Lord Jesus Christ*, and the love of *God*, and the fellowship of the *Holy Spirit* be with you all. (2 Cor. 13:14)

A Closer Look—Galatians 4:4–6

For our focal passage, let's look at Paul's encouraging words in Galatians 4:4–6. (NOTE: *Abba* is italic in NIV.)

[4]But when the time had fully come, *God* sent his *Son*, born of

a woman, born under law, [5]to redeem those under law, that we

might receive the full rights of sons. [6]Because you are sons,

God sent the *Spirit* of his *Son* into our hearts, the *Spirit* who

calls out, "*Abba*, Father."

The word **trinity** is never found in the Bible, but this does not mean that the concept of a triune God is absent from the Bible. Our beliefs are sometimes based on concepts that are bigger than single words.

Do you know of an analogy or two that can help you understand God as Trinity?

SCRIPTURE NOTES

Do you see any problems with analogies that help us understand God as Trinity?

1. Look up Galatians in your study Bible, and read about this letter. What are some of the main issues that Paul is confronting in his letter to the Galatians?

2. Read what comes before and after 4:4–6, and write down anything that helps you understand the context and meaning of this text.

3. Mark your observations of 4:4–6 below. Look for time references, lists, purpose statements, result statements, explanations, the actions of God, and so on.

But when the time had fully come,

God sent his Son, born of a woman,

born under law, to redeem those

under law, that we might receive

the full rights of sons. Because

you are sons, God sent the Spirit

of his Son into our hearts, the Spirit

who calls out, "Abba, Father."

4. How do you see the triune nature of God revealed in Galatians 4:4–6?

So What?

1. Groups that deny the doctrine of the Trinity have historically been considered cults. Why is believing in God as Trinity such a big deal? What would happen if you denied either the oneness of God or the deity of the Father, Son, or Spirit?

2. How do you personally experience each person of the Trinity?

3. Does viewing God as Trinity change your view of God in any way?

4. In some ways we can say that "God *is* community" (eternal three-in-one relationship of giving to others). What does God's being community say about the importance of fellowship or community for us?

Mutual Submission

The function of one member [person] of the Trinity may for a time be subordinate to one or both of the other members, but that does not mean he is in any way inferior in essence. Each of the three persons of the Trinity has had, for a period of time, a particular function unique to himself. This is to be understood as a temporary role for the purpose of accomplishing a given end, not a change in his status or essence.

—Millard J. Erickson,
Christian Theology, 338

Cross-References
Matt. 3:16–17; 28:19–20; John 1:33–34; 14:16, 26; 16:13–15; 20:21–22; Rom. 15:16; 1 Cor. 12:4–6; 2 Cor. 1:21–22; 13:14; Gal. 4:6; Rev. 1:4–5

For Deeper Study
Erickson, Millard J. *Christian Theology.* 2nd ed. Grand Rapids: Baker, 1998.

McGrath, Alister E. *Understanding the Trinity.* Grand Rapids: Zondervan, 1988.

Olson, Roger E. *The Mosaic of Christian Belief.* Downers Grove, IL: InterVarsity Press, 2002.

White, James R. *The Forgotten Trinity: Recovering the Heart of Christian Belief.* Minneapolis: Bethany House, 1998.

Life Together

Fellowshiping

Even if you and I (or any other human being) had never been born, God would still live in perfect community: Father, Son, and Spirit, three-in-one, one-in-three, living in eternal fellowship. Have you ever stopped to think about what that means for us? By making us in his image, God created in us a deep need for fellowship. As we experience the God who invented fellowship, we can expect him to draw us into deeper relationships with our friends in Christ. In Behaving 2 we will look at the habit of fellowship—living in authentic relationship with and dependence upon Jesus Christ and those who follow him.

Fellowship is both a *fact* of the Christian life and a *habit* or practice of the Christian life. It's like being a member of a family (fact) and then getting together with that family (habit), or being part of the church (fact) and then gathering with the church (habit). When it comes to fellowship, the fact or reality of fellowship makes possible the habit or practice.

Dietrich Bonhoeffer, the faithful German pastor who was hanged in a Nazi concentration camp just days before the Allies liberated the camp, wrote a classic book about fellowship called *Life Together*. He reminds us that fellowship is above all a new relationship we have with God and with other believers that is made possible by the death and resurrection of Jesus Christ and made personal and real by the presence of the Holy Spirit (2 Cor. 13:14; Phil. 2:1). Bonhoeffer stresses that "we belong to one another only through and in Jesus Christ" (*Life Together*, 21). There is no fellowship with God or with other Christians apart from Christ.

The apostle Paul says as much in 1 Corinthians 1:9—"God, who has called you into fellowship with his Son Jesus Christ our Lord, is faithful." John spells it out in even more detail.

The life [Jesus] appeared; we have seen it and testify to it, and we proclaim to you the eternal life, which was with the Father and has appeared to us. We proclaim to you what we have seen and heard, so that you also may have *fellowship* with us. And our *fellowship* is with the Father and with his Son, Jesus Christ. . . . This is the message we have heard from him and declare to you: God is light; in him there is no darkness at all. If we claim to have *fellowship* with him yet walk in the darkness, we lie and do not live by the truth. But if we walk in the light, as he is in the light, we have *fellowship* with one another, and the blood of Jesus, his Son, purifies us from all sin. (1 John 1:2–3, 5–7)

The New Testament uses different words to emphasize the fact or reality of fellowship. We are *partners* with other Christians in the cause of the gospel (Phil. 1:5; Philem. 17). We may even *participate* in the sufferings of Christ (Phil. 3:10; 1 Peter 4:13). As Christians, we refuse to *share* in the sins of others or *participate* with evil powers (1 Cor. 10:18, 20; 1 Tim. 5:22; 2 John 11).

The most noticeable fellowship habit in the New Testament is that of meeting practical needs. Christians living in authentic relationship with and dependence upon Jesus Christ will make it a priority to meet the needs of fellow Christians. The italicized words in the following verses are the English translations of Greek words for "fellowship":

Share with God's people who are in need. Practice hospitality. (Rom. 12:13)

For Macedonia and Achaia were pleased to make a *contribution* for the poor among the saints in Jerusalem. They were pleased to do it, and indeed they owe it to them. For if the Gentiles have *shared* in the Jews' spiritual blessings, they owe it to the Jews to *share* with them their material blessings. (Rom. 15:26–27)

For I testify that they gave as much as they were able, and even beyond their ability. Entirely on their own, they urgently pleaded with us for the privilege of *sharing* in this service to the saints. (2 Cor. 8:3–4)

Because of the service by which you have proved yourselves, men will praise God for the obedience that accompanies your confession of the gospel of Christ, and for your generosity in *sharing* with them and with everyone else. (2 Cor. 9:13)

Anyone who receives instruction in the word must *share* all good things with his instructor. (Gal. 6:6)

Moreover, as you Philippians know, in the early days of your acquaintance with the gospel, when I set out from Macedonia, not

Inspect Your Heart Before You Take the Lord's Supper?

You've probably heard preachers warn you to examine your heart carefully before you dare take the Lord's Supper based on Paul's warning to the Corinthian Christians:

Therefore, whoever eats the bread or drinks the cup of the Lord in an unworthy manner will be guilty of sinning against the body and blood of the Lord. A man ought to examine himself before he eats of the bread and drinks of the cup. For anyone who eats and drinks without recognizing the body of the Lord eats and drinks judgment on himself. (1 Cor. 11:27–29)

The best of evangelical scholarship suggests that some Corinthians were sinning by failing to use their material resources to meet the practical needs of others in their church. They were failing at fellowship. Craig Blomberg writes,

Many Christians have entirely missed the real meaning of these threats, which, . . . are directed against those who are not adequately loving their Christian brothers and sisters and providing for their physical or material needs. . . . [Paul's] warning was not to those who were leading unworthy lives and longed for forgiveness. . . . [Rather, his warning was this]—Those who eat and drink in flagrant disregard of the physical needs of others in their fellowship risk incurring the punishment of God. (*1 Corinthians*, 231–33)

God is very concerned with how his children treat each other, and not even the Lord's Supper can be used as an excuse to neglect each other's needs.

"apostles' teaching"—This phrase probably refers to the teachings of Jesus passed down through his apostles. These teachings likely focused on the life, ministry, teachings, death, and resurrection of Jesus, along with the response to this good news and the Spirit's work through the church. Today this authoritative teaching is accessible in the New Testament.

"fellowship"—In the New Testament period, the word *koinōnia* (fellowship) was used of business partnerships in which people were connected through work. It was also a favorite expression to describe the marriage relationship. The basic idea of the word involves generosity in sharing, giving, or participating.

"breaking of bread"—This expression probably has a double significance. First, it refers to sharing a meal in a home. Second, it also refers to the Christian practice of taking the Lord's Supper as part of that ordinary fellowship meal.

one church *shared* with me in the matter of giving and receiving, except you only; for even when I was in Thessalonica, you sent me aid again and again when I was in need. (Phil. 4:15–16)

Command those who are rich in this present world not to be arrogant nor to put their hope in wealth, which is so uncertain, but to put their hope in God, who richly provides us with everything for our enjoyment. Command them to do good, to be rich in good deeds, and to be generous and *willing to share*. (1 Tim. 6:17–18)

And do not forget to do good and to *share* with others, for with such sacrifices God is pleased. (Heb. 13:16)

Kent Hughes helps us to see that the biblical reality of fellowship always involves giving:

Fellowship is not just a sentimental feeling of oneness. It is not punch and cookies. It does not take place simply because we are in the church ["fellowship"] hall. Fellowship comes through *giving*. True fellowship costs! So many people never know the joys of Christian fellowship because they have never learned to give themselves away. . . . Do you want to have fellowship? You must be a giver. (*Acts: The Church Afire*, 49)

A Closer Look—Acts 2:42–47

The first two chapters of Acts are packed with unusual and exciting information about the early church. The final paragraph of chapter 2 sums up the condition of the church in those very early days and makes it clear that fellowship was at the heart of the life of the early church.

[42]They [the church] devoted themselves to the apostles' teaching and to the fellowship, to the breaking of bread and to prayer. [43]Everyone was filled with awe, and many wonders and miraculous signs were done by the apostles. [44]All the believers were together and had everything in common. [45]Selling their possessions and goods, they gave to anyone as he had need. [46]Every day they continued to meet together in the temple courts. They broke bread in their homes and ate together with glad and

sincere hearts, [47]praising God and enjoying the favor of all the people. And the Lord added to their number daily those who were being saved.

The questions below may help you grasp the meaning of Acts 2:42–47.

1. Those first Christians devoted themselves to four things (v. 42). What were they?

2. What would be the contemporary equivalent of these four things? (See "The Power of Words" for help.)

3. Not everything in 2:43–47 relates to fellowship, but much of it does. What do you see in the rest of this paragraph that helps you understand how the first Christians experienced true fellowship?

Crossing the Bridge

How does our situation differ from the early church situation described in Acts 2:42–47?

- We cannot meet together in the temple courts (v. 46).

-

-

Community and Solitude

Let him who cannot be alone beware of community. He will only do harm to himself and to the community. Alone you stood before God when he called you; alone you had to answer that call; alone you had to struggle and pray; and alone you will die and give an account to God. You cannot escape from yourself; for God singled you out. . . .

But the reverse is also true: *Let him who is not in community beware of being alone.* Into the community you were called, the call was not meant for you alone; in the community of the called you bear your cross, you struggle, you pray. You are not alone, even in death, and on the Last Day you will be only one member of the great congregation of Jesus Christ.

We recognize, then, that only as we are within the fellowship can we be alone, and only he that is alone can live in the fellowship.

—Dietrich Bonhoeffer,
Life Together, 77

Cross-References
Look back over the references cited throughout Behaving 2.

For Deeper Study
Bolinger, Tod E. *It Takes a Church to Raise a Christian.* Grand Rapids: Brazos, 2004.
Bonhoeffer, Dietrich. *Life Together.* San Francisco: HarperSanFrancisco, 1954.
Ortberg, John. *Everybody's Normal Till You Get to Know Them.* Grand Rapids: Zondervan, 2003.
Wilson, Jonathan R. *Why Church Matters: Worship, Ministry, and Mission in Practice.* Grand Rapids: Brazos, 2006.

What theological principles do you see in Acts 2:42–47 that tell us what fellowship is and how we can experience it? (Remember, theological principles should apply equally well to the biblical audience and to us.)

• We can be together and not experience fellowship, but we can't experience fellowship if we do not spend time together (principle from v. 44).

•

•

So What?

1. How does fellowship relate to friendship?

2. When you are with other Christians, what do you spend time doing?

3. How much time do you spend with other Christians devoting yourselves to the study of the Bible, to prayer, to community building, to meeting practical needs, and to worship?

4. Do you know anybody in your church with financial or other practical needs? How would you ever find out if people had such needs in our society?

5. What are some ways that God might be calling you to use your time and money to meet the practical needs of other Christians?

6. Do you personally have practical needs that your community group could meet?

The Greatest of These

Love

God is Trinity—Father, Son, and Spirit living in an eternal relationship of self-giving love. God wants us to experience this community of love with him. We need him, and we need each other. We've seen how fellowship is both a reality we enter into when we are joined to Christ and a habit of giving to other believers. When we accept God's invitation to join his community, we begin to open our hearts and hands and let his love flow through us to meet the practical needs of others. When we become passionately consumed with giving to others and doing what God says is best for them, our lives will be characterized by love. In Becoming 2 we will look at the character quality of love, the king of the virtues—"the greatest of these."

Love is what holds us together in the messy, nitty-gritty of life as a community. We sometimes enter a community with our own dream or vision of what that community should be like. Then we meet that irritating person, or things don't go our way, or the decision is made without us, or something else happens that challenges our perfect ideal of community. God begins to shatter our dream and our ideal and replace it with his reality and truth. At that point we have a choice to make—either we hand over our dreams to God, or we continue to fight for our own vision of community. Dietrich Bonhoeffer offers a sobering warning about this important choice.

Every human wish dream that is injected into the Christian community is a hindrance to genuine community and must be banished if genuine community is to survive. He who loves his dream of a community more than the Christian community itself becomes a

What is the difference between being un-loved and being unlovable?

Love Takes a Risk

To love at all is to be vulnerable. Love anything, and your heart will certainly be wrung and possibly be broken. If you want to make sure of keeping it intact, you must give your heart to no one, not even to an animal. . . . The only place outside Heaven where you can be perfectly safe from all the dangers . . . of love is Hell.

—C. S. Lewis,
The Four Loves, 111–12

destroyer of the latter, even though his personal intentions may be ever so honest and earnest and sacrificial. (*Life Together*, 27)

What is your vision, or "wish dream," for your community? Are you willing to sacrifice your dream so that God may give you his dream?

The Bible speaks often about love (see the many cross-references on page 47). In 1 Corinthians 13:4–7 the apostle Paul defines what biblical love is and what it is not.

> Love is patient, love is kind. It does not envy, it does not boast, it is not proud. It is not rude, it is not self-seeking, it is not easily angered, it keeps no record of wrongs. Love does not delight in evil but rejoices with the truth. It always protects, always trusts, always hopes, always perseveres.

In the original language Paul uses fifteen verbs in this passage to define love. Instead of "love is patient" or "love is kind," the idea is more like "love acts with patience" or "love shows kindness." Love is an action before it is an emotion. This means that we can love people we don't even like. The story below reminds us that love is primarily a choice.

> Newspaper columnist and minister George Crane tells of a wife who came into his office full of hatred toward her husband. "I do not only want to get rid of him; I want to get even. Before I divorce him, I want to hurt him as much as he has me." Dr. Crane suggested an ingenious plan. "Go home and act as if you really loved your husband. Tell him how much he means to you. Praise him for every decent trait. Go out of your way to be as kind, considerate, and generous as possible. Spare no efforts to please him, to enjoy him. Make him believe that you love him. After you've convinced him of your undying love and that you cannot live without him, then drop the bomb. Tell him that you're getting a divorce. That will really hurt him." With revenge in her eyes, she smiled and exclaimed, "Beautiful, beautiful. Will he ever be surprised!" And she did it with enthusiasm. Acting "as if." For two months she showed love, kindness, listening, giving, reinforcing, sharing. When she didn't return, Crane called. "Are you ready now to go through with the divorce?" "Divorce!" she exclaimed. "Never! I discovered I really do love him." Her actions had changed her feelings. Motion resulted in emotion. The ability to love is established not so much by fervent promise as often repeated deeds. (Larson, *Illustrations*, 137)

Love is a choice to do what God says is best for another person.

Only God's love flowing through us will keep us bound together in fellowship. Yet there is a lot of confusion about what love really means, even among Christians. What are some common ways our culture defines "love" that are different from the Bible's definition?

A Closer Look—1 John 4:7–8

Our focal passage in this study is 1 John 4:7–8. Mark up the passage below with your observations. Look for important words, commands, contrasts, purpose statements, result statements, pronouns, conjunctions, emotional terms, and so on.

SCRIPTURE NOTES

7aBeloved, let us love one another,

7bfor love is from God;

7cand everyone who loves is born of God and knows God.

8aThe one who does not love does not know God,

8bfor God is love. (NASB)

1. Look at the context of the text. Begin by reading the introduction to 1 John in a study Bible. Why does John emphasize the theme of love in this letter?

2. Since a new section probably starts at verse 7, the immediate context of our passage is 4:7–12. Read these verses, and jot down what they teach us about love.

   • 4:7–8

   • 4:9–10

   • 4:11–12

Jesus' Final Words
On the night before he was crucified, Jesus talked a lot about love. People usually don't waste words right before they die. Read John 13–15 and summarize what Jesus is teaching us about love.

Letting God Love Us
I will love God because he first loved me. I will obey God because I love God. But if I cannot accept God's love, I cannot love him in return, and I cannot obey him. Self-discipline will never make us feel righteous or clean; accepting God's love will.

—Don Miller,
Blue Like Jazz, 86

Does the New Testament really have one word for human love and another word for God's kind of love? There are two main words for love (*agapē* and *phileō*), but it may surprise you to learn that both words can be used for human love and for God's kind of love. See for yourself:

God's kind of love

- "God so loved [*agapē*] the world" (John 3:16)
- "The Father loves [*phileō*] the Son" (John 5:20)

Human love

- "Men loved [*agapē*] darkness instead of light" (John 3:19)
- The Pharisees "love [*phileō*] the place of honor at banquets" (Matt. 23:6)

In reality, these words are interchangeable. Both can be used for human love, and both can be used for God's kind of love. Context rather than dictionary definitions determines the meaning of a word.

Write your favorite quote about biblical love:

---

3. What is the key command (v. 7a)?

4. What are the two reasons that we should obey the command (vv. 7b, 8b)?

5. When the Bible says that "God is love" (v. 8b), is that the same as saying that "love is God"? What does "God is love" mean?

6. What is the result of carrying out the command? The result is stated both positively (4:7c) and negatively (4:8a).

7. Why does John say "knows God" rather than "knows about God"?

Crossing the Bridge

Write a present-tense statement that captures the theological heart of 1 John 4:7–8. In this case the "river" separating us from the biblical audience is neither wide nor deep.

So What?

1. What is the most important thing God seems to be saying to you through 1 John 4:7–8?

2. In your own words, explain the connection between Trinity, fellowshiping (or community), and love.

3. Who is the most loving human being you know? What are some specific things that person has done to show love to you and to others?

4. What is the difference between saying "Emily is loving" and "God is love"?

5. What are the greatest obstacles to love in your life?

6. What are three specific things you can do this week to cultivate biblical love in your life?

Cross-References (a partial list)
Matt. 5:44; Luke 10:25–37; John 3:16; 13:34–35; 14:15, 21, 23; 15:9–10; 21:15–17; Rom. 5:5, 8; 8:31–39; 12:9; 13:8–10; 1 Cor. 13; Gal. 5:13–15, 22; Eph. 3:14–19; 5:1–2; Col. 3:14; 1 Peter 4:8; 1 John 3:11–18; 4:7–21

For Deeper Study
Lewis, C. S. *The Four Loves.* Glasgow: William Collins, 1960.
Ortberg, John. *Love Beyond Reason: Moving God's Love from Your Head to Your Heart.* Grand Rapids: Zondervan, 1998.
Smedes, Lewis B. *Love Within Limits.* Grand Rapids: Eerdmans, 1978.
Yancey, Philip. *What's So Amazing About Grace?* Grand Rapids: Zondervan, 1997.

Our Father in Heaven

Great and Good God

Growing up Baptist, our mealtime prayers were short, sweet, and rarely the same. The adults in my circle sometimes fell into prayer ruts, and those ruts normally focused on food as much as on God—"Bless this food to the nourishment of our bodies and our bodies to Thy service." In contrast, the mealtime prayers of my liturgical Lutheran cousins were always the same—"God is great, God is good, let us thank him for our food. Amen." As a child in one faith tradition listening to the prayers of children in another tradition, their single mealtime prayer seemed repetitive, boring, and meaningless. Repetitive—yes; boring—maybe; but meaningless—never. This simple childhood prayer captures the very heart of what Christians have always believed about who God is.

God Is Great

Christians claim that God is both great and good. On the one hand, God is great, transcendent (far removed), holy, infinite, powerful, majestic, sovereign, and independent. Many, many passages of Scripture confirm God's greatness. Here are just a few.

> Who among the gods is like you, O LORD? Who is like you—majestic in holiness, awesome in glory, working wonders? (Exod. 15:11)

> I am the LORD who brought you up out of Egypt to be your God; therefore be holy, because I am holy. (Lev. 11:45)

> With man this is impossible, but not with God; all things are possible with God. (Mark 10:27)

> The God who made the world and everything in it is the Lord of heaven and earth and does not live in temples built by hands. And he is not served by human hands, as if he needed anything, because he himself gives all men life and breath and everything else. (Acts 17:24–25)

Nothing in all creation is hidden from God's sight. Everything is uncovered and laid bare before the eyes of him to whom we must give account. (Heb. 4:13)

God Is Good

On the other hand, God is good, imminent (close or near), loving, gracious, merciful, compassionate, self-sacrificing, kind, and faithful. He is not an impersonal force, but a person who invites us into an intimate relationship. Scripture also affirms God's goodness.

> Know therefore that the LORD your God is God; he is the faithful God, keeping his covenant of love to a thousand generations of those who love him and keep his commands." (Deut. 7:9)

> But you, O Lord, are a compassionate and gracious God, slow to anger, abounding in love and faithfulness. (Ps. 86:15)

> Give thanks to the LORD, for he is good. His love endures forever. (Ps. 136:1)

The God revealed to us in the Bible is both great and good. Since *God is great*, he can do something about the suffering and evil in the world. He can rescue people from their sins. He can answer prayer, perform miracles, and bring about a final victory over evil.

Since *God is good*, he gets involved in a personal way with his creation. He is available and near. He enters into a covenant relationship with us, understands our weaknesses, and responds compassionately to our needs.

A Closer Look—Matthew 6:9

At the very center of Jesus' Sermon on the Mount stands the "Lord's Prayer" (Matt. 6:9–15). The prayer begins very simply, "Our Father in heaven." This brief expression summarizes God's character as a great and good God.

Our Father

Throughout the Old Testament, God is portrayed as the "Father" of Israel—"When Israel was a child, I loved him, and out of Egypt I called my son" (Hos. 11:1). It was rare, however, to find individual Israelites addressing God as "Father." God was the Father of the nation.

When Jesus arrived on the scene, he made the bold claim that God was his Father—"All things have been handed over to Me by My Father; and no one knows the Son except the Father; nor does anyone know the Father except the Son, and anyone to whom the Son wills to reveal Him" (Matt. 11:27 NASB). Jesus used the expression "My Father" as his primary way of addressing God. Jesus never referred to "our Father" (in Matthew 6:9 he is teaching *us* how to pray) since his sonship is absolutely unique and different

Notice what happens when we deny either God's greatness or his goodness:

Deism—A view of God that portrays him as creating the world but then not getting involved with the world. He is the designer of the universe but not intimately or personally involved with his creation. The deist god may be compared to an absentee landlord. He started the project and then abandoned it. The deist god doesn't answer prayer, perform miracles, or relate personally with his creation. He is great but not good.

Panentheism—A view of God that overemphasizes God's goodness to the neglect of his greatness. God and the world are not identical, but God is dependent on the world. Without the world, God could not be God, according to this view. The panentheist god is always in the process of becoming god. He is the fellow sufferer who loves, cares, and understands, but he is not sovereign, in control, or all-powerful. God is good but not great.

How does Psalm 145 reveal God's greatness and goodness?

I will exalt you, my God the King; I will praise your name for ever and ever. Every day I will praise you and extol your name for ever and ever. Great is the Lord and most worthy of praise; his greatness no one can fathom. One generation will commend your works to another; they will tell of your mighty acts. They will speak of the glorious splendor of your majesty, and I will meditate on your wonderful works. They will tell of the power of your awesome works, and I will proclaim your great deeds. They will celebrate your abundant goodness and joyfully sing of your righteousness. The Lord is gracious and compassionate, slow to anger and rich in love. The Lord is good to all; he has compassion on all he has made. All you have made will praise you, O Lord; your saints will extol you. They will tell of the glory of your kingdom and speak of your might, so that all men may know of your mighty acts and the glorious splendor of your kingdom. Your kingdom is an everlasting kingdom, and your dominion endures through all generations. The Lord is faithful to all his promises and loving toward all he has made. The Lord upholds all those who fall and lifts up all who are bowed down. The eyes of all look to you, and you give them their food at the proper time. You open your hand and satisfy the desires of every living thing. The Lord is righteous in all his ways and loving toward all he has made. The Lord is near to all who call on him, to all who call on him in truth. He fulfills the desires of those who fear him; he hears their cry and saves them. The Lord watches over all who love him, but all the wicked he will destroy. My mouth will speak in praise of the Lord. Let every creature praise his holy name for ever and ever.

from ours. Jesus is the Son by nature; we are sons and daughters by adoption. He is the Son by right; we are sons and daughters by grace. He says "My Father"; we say "our Father." What is amazing is that Jesus teaches his disciples to call God "Father." As adopted children, we cry "Abba! Father!"

> For you did not receive a spirit that makes you a slave again to fear, but you received the Spirit of sonship. And by him we cry, *"Abba, Father."* The Spirit himself testifies with our spirit that we are God's children. (Rom. 8:15–16)

What does it mean to you that Jesus instructs you to call God "Father"?

The title "Father" indicates that God desires an intimate, personal relationship with you. God's goodness and tenderness come through when Jesus gives you permission to address God in this way.

Frederick Bruner helps us see this even more clearly.

> The "our" [in "Our Father"] means belonging, mercy, home. It is a *possessive* pronoun meaning that God the Father is ours and we are his. In the "our" is contained the joy of the whole gospel. We will never be able to calculate the honor that has been done us by being allowed to pray "Our Father." (*Christbook*, 239)

Think a bit more about what our Father does for us:

- Our Father rewards us for "secret service" (Matt. 6:3–4, 6, 17–18)
- Our Father knows what we need before we ask him (Matt. 6:8)
- Our Father will meet our needs (Matt. 6:32–34)
- Our Father has prepared an inheritance for us (Matt. 25:34; Col. 1:12)
- Our Father is merciful (Luke 6:36)
- Our Father loves us, whether we are unrighteous or self-righteous (Luke 15:11–32)
- Our Father seeks our worship (John 4:23–24)
- Our Father protects us from spiritual harm (John 10:29; 17:11)
- Our Father comforts us (2 Cor. 1:3–4)
- Our Father has given us the Holy Spirit (John 14:16, 26; Gal. 4:4–6)
- Our Father has blessed us with every spiritual blessing in Christ (Eph. 1:3)
- Our Father has given us new life (1 Peter 1:3)
- Our Father loves us (1 John 3:1)

In Heaven

God is not only "Our Father," he is our Father "in heaven." We tend to become too familiar with God in our culture. God is often addressed in ways that are informal to the point of being irreverent. You have probably heard that the Aramaic word *abba* meant "Daddy." In the 1960s a scholar named Joachim Jeremias popularized this view, but his scholarship was flawed. Later, after being corrected by other scholars, Jeremias himself admitted his mistake, but not before preachers had picked up the idea that *abba* was a child's tender word for daddy and encouraged us to call God "Daddy." The word *abba* was used by children, but it was also used by adults to speak to their fathers. "Abba" (which isn't used in the Lord's Prayer) simply means father and should be translated "Father," not "Daddy." Jesus teaches us that real prayer begins with a respectful awe of the Lord.

Just because God is good and wants an intimate relationship with us doesn't mean that we should lose sight of his greatness. He is our Father "in heaven." He is high and lifted up. He is the almighty Creator of heaven and earth. He is the sovereign King of the universe. To him belongs all glory and honor and power. He is seated on the throne of heaven, and we should approach him with awe and reverence.

What can you do to deepen your reverence for God?

Great prayers reveal a great awareness of God. Jesus teaches us to pray, "Our Father in heaven." God desires an intimate, personal relationship with us because he is "our Father" and he has adopted us in Christ. Because he is our Father "in heaven," we bow before him in humility and respect. The childhood mealtime prayer of my Lutheran cousins got it right. God is both great and good. When we have a biblical, balanced view of God's nature as both great and good, we will want to thank him for our food, for our lives, for everything. We call that worship, and that is the habit that flows out of trusting in our great and good God.

Adoption

We biological parents know well the earnest longing to have a child. But in many cases our cribs were filled easily. We decided to have a child and a child came. . . . I've heard of unplanned pregnancies, but I've never heard of an unplanned adoption. That's why adoptive parents understand God's passion to adopt us. They know what it means to feel an empty space inside. They know what it means to hunt, to set out on a mission, and take responsibility for a child with a spotted past and a dubious future. If anybody understands God's ardor for his children, it's someone who has rescued an orphan from despair, for that is what God has done for us. God has adopted you. God sought you, found you, signed the papers and took you home.

—Max Lucado,
The Great House of God, 15

Cross-References (a partial list)

Job 38:1–42:6; Psalm 23; 89; 104; 107; Isa. 6:1–7; Matt. 5:48; Mark 14:35–36; Rom. 8:15–16; 2 Cor. 1:3–4; Gal. 4:6; Heb. 12:3–11; Rev. 4–5

For Deeper Study

Carson, D. A. *The Sermon on the Mount: An Evangelical Exposition of Matthew 5–7.* Grand Rapids: Baker, 1978.

Dodd, Brian J. *Praying Jesus' Way.* Downers Grove, IL: InterVarsity Press, 1997.

Lucado, Max. *The Great House of God.* Dallas: Word, 1997.

Olson, Roger E. *The Mosaic of Christian Belief.* Downers Grove, IL: InterVarsity Press, 2002.

So What?

1. What is the most dominant picture of God in your mind? A grandfather? An authority figure? A best friend?

2. In what ways has your relationship with your earthly parents shaped your view of God?

3. More than anything else, what helps you sense that God wants to draw you close and enjoy an intimate relationship with you as your loving Father?

4. On the other hand, what helps you recognize and stand in awe of God's holiness, mighty power, and glorious majesty?

5. Are you drawn more to God's greatness or goodness? What do you need to do to move toward a more balanced understanding of God as both great and good?

Come, Let Us Bow Down

Worshiping

"God is great, God is good, let us thank him . . ." This children's prayer confesses God's character as holy, majestic, and powerful but also as loving, gracious, and merciful. While God is enthroned on high as the sovereign Creator of the universe, he is also our Father, who knows us by name and longs for our companionship. The unapproachable Light has chosen to come near as our Friend. The belief that God is both great and good leads us to respond with praise, gratitude, and obedience. In other words, when we see ourselves for who we are and God for who he is, we bow down. In Behaving 3, we will take a closer look at the habit of Christian worship—the one thing we were all created for.

High and lofty realities are hard to define because they resist being reduced to a few words. Worship falls into that category. We should try to define worship (see Louie Giglio's helpful definition on page 56), but we shouldn't be surprised if our attempts fall short. In fact, describing worship is often more helpful than trying to define it. For instance, authentic Christian worship . . .

- never starts with us. God begins worship by creating us, loving us, and blessing us. Everything we do in worship begins with God.
- is our response to God for who he is and what he has done. This involves praise, thanksgiving, gratitude, reverence, and many other things.
- is holistic, involving all of us (i.e., what we think, say, and do) in all of life, not just on Sunday mornings.

"Sing to the Lord a New Song" (Pss. 93–100)

Take time this week to read these magnificent psalms of worship. As you read and reflect on these psalms, consider . . .

- What is God like?
- What has God done for you?
- How are we supposed to respond to God?
- How is God calling us to worship him?

SCRIPTURE NOTES

- is both personal and corporate. Our worship will never be complete unless we connect with a local body of believers to honor and exalt the Lord together.
- includes obedience. Gathering with other believers is just one aspect of offering ourselves to God as living, holy, and pleasing sacrifices.

Even better than defining or describing worship is experiencing worship. If you want to grow and mature in this habit, you need to connect with a local church and participate in corporate worship. What should you look for when trying to find a community that worships biblically? The New Testament consistently identifies six essential elements of Christian worship:

- Praise (Eph. 5:18–20; Col. 3:16)
- Prayers (Acts 2:42; 4:24; 1 Tim. 2:1–2; James 5:16)
- Scripture reading (Col. 4:16; 1 Thess. 5:27; 1 Tim. 4:13)
- Teaching and exhortation from Scripture (2 Tim. 4:1–4; Tit. 2:15; Heb. 10:24–25)
- Giving an offering (1 Cor. 16:1–2; 2 Cor. 8:1–8; 9:6–13)
- Baptism and the Lord's Supper (ordinances) (Matt. 26:26–29; 28:18–20; Acts 2:38–41; 1 Cor. 11:20–34)

All six elements are extremely significant and serve to enrich our personal encounter with God, but unless his Spirit touches our spirit, we have not truly worshiped (see the Foster quote on page 56).

A Closer Look—Psalm 100

Our focal passage in this study is Psalm 100.

¹Shout for joy to the LORD, all the earth.

²Worship the LORD with gladness; come before him with joyful songs.

³Know that the LORD is God. It is he who made us, and we are his;

we are his people, the sheep of his pasture.

⁴Enter his gates with thanksgiving and his courts with praise;

give thanks to him and praise his name.

⁵For the LORD is good and his love endures forever;

his faithfulness continues through all generations.

Psalm 100 serves as the dramatic conclusion to a series of hymns celebrating God's greatness and goodness (93–99). This hymn was sung during one of the Jewish festivals as people gathered to recognize God as King over all the earth. Use the questions below to dig deeper into Psalm 100.

1. What are the seven commands in verses 1–4?

2. What is the central command (v. 3)? Why is this command foundational to the other six commands? (Hint: Look carefully at the explanation in v. 3b.)

3. What are the attitudes or actions of worship (e.g., "with gladness" or "with praise")?

4. What are the reasons for worship (see v. 5)?

5. What does this psalm tell us about who we are? What does it tell us about who God is? How does true worship connect these two?

Crossing the Bridge

What are the differences between the biblical audience and us? For example, when we gather for worship, we don't enter the gates or courts of the Old Testament temple. Do you notice any other differences?

Making the Most of Corporate Worship

Worship is much more than just gathering with other Christians to pray, give money, sing praises, hear scriptural teaching, and celebrate baptism and the Lord's Supper. Worship is a relational encounter with God rather than a set of religious rituals. If we never let God break through to us, we will find it difficult to respond to him. Think about the priority you place on corporate worship.

How do you prepare for worship?

What hinders you from worshiping?

Where does corporate worship rank in priority right now in your life?

Cross-References

Exod. 3:1–6; Deut. 6; Psalms (the entire book); Isa. 6:1–6; Malachi (the entire book); John 4:1–26; Rom. 12:1–2; Heb. 12:28–29; 13:15–16; James 4:7–10; Rev. 4–5, 19–21

For Deeper Study

Beach, Nancy. *An Hour on Sunday: Creating Moments of Transformation and Wonder.* Grand Rapids: Zondervan, 2004.

Foster, Richard J. *Celebration of Discipline.* 25th anniversary ed. San Francisco: HarperSanFrancisco, 2003.

Giglio, Louie. *The Air I Breathe: Worship as a Way of Life.* Sisters, OR: Multnomah, 2003.

Peterson, David. *Engaging with God: A Biblical Theology of Worship.* Downers Grove, IL: InterVarsity Press, 1992.

Rognlien, Bob. *Experiential Worship: Encountering God with Heart, Soul, Mind and Strength.* Colorado Springs: NavPress, 2005.

What are the timeless theological principles in Psalm 100 that connect with both the biblical audience and with us (the bridge between their time and ours)?

So What?

1. What is your favorite definition of worship?

2. Which New Testament elements of worship does your local church emphasize the most? Which ones would you like to emphasize more in corporate worship?

3. What have been some of your most memorable corporate worship experiences?

4. How important are worship forms or styles to you? Why?

5. What do you need to do to deepen your worship of the great and good God?

6. What are two specific ways that you can live out the message of Psalm 100 this week?

BEHAVING 3—*Worshiping*

Be Holy, Because I Am Holy

Purity

The belief that God is both great and good—"our Father in heaven"—calls for the only appropriate response to God's "overture of love"—the habit of worship. Worship is "our response, both personal and corporate, to God—for who He is and what He has done expressed in and by the things we say and the way we live" (Louie Giglio, *The Air I Breathe,* 49). Our response should be more than a Sunday morning, lifting-voices, raising-hands, praying-prayers response. Gathering with other believers to worship is crucial to a healthy spiritual life, but we worship primarily by how we live. The habit of whole-life worship nurtures in us the character quality of purity—living a holy life in public and private that honors God.

In the spring of 1995, revival broke out on many college campuses across America. One characteristic of this visitation from God was students dealing with sinful habits that they had previously let linger in their lives. Bonne Steffen interviewed several students for *The Christian Reader.* One student named Brian at Asbury College said:

> I was a leader on campus. We had invited Wheaton students to come and share. At first, I was praying for other people, but then I began to think about my own struggles. I stood in line for three hours with one of my best friends all the time thinking, *How can I get up there and admit I'm less than perfect?* But I also realized that being on a Christian campus isn't protection from the world. I have really struggled with lust. I found I wasn't alone. It was an issue for a lot of others. Personally, I wanted the chain to be broken; I wanted that stuff

out of my life. If it meant no magazines, no television, I was willing to eliminate them. A number of us signed a paper stating our desire for purity, which we put in a box and placed on the altar. I'm still accountable to other people. My deepest desire is to be pure in my heart and thoughts. (Larson, *Choice Contemporary Stories*, 217)

Brian was busy serving God as a ministry leader but was not ready to admit he needed God's help in his own life. He discovered, however, that God cares as much about his character as his ministry. What was the turning point for Brian?

Things begin to happen in our lives when it dawns on us that God cares as much about *working in* our lives as he does about *working through* our lives.

Be Holy?

God is utterly pure and perfect. He is distinct and separate from everything he created and all other competing gods. We need a word to describe how God's very being is different from anything we know—our word is *holy*. In other words, God defines holiness; it is not the other way around. (By the way, the words translated "pure" and "holy" in our New Testaments come from the same word family in Greek.)

A common name for God in the Old Testament is the "Holy One" (Isa. 40:25; 43:15; Ezek. 39:7; Hos. 11:9). People, places, and things are "holy" only because they are in contact with God, who alone is holy. That closeness to God explains why in the Old Testament the tabernacle and temple are considered holy. That connection also helps us understand why a common New Testament description for those who belong to God is "holy ones" (normally translated "saints"). God's people are holy because they belong to God, are connected to God, and are close to God.

When we enter a relationship with God through Jesus Christ, we are given God's Holy Spirit, and our physical bodies become the temple of the Holy Spirit (1 Cor. 6:19). In this sense, we have already become holy (i.e., indwelt by the Holy Spirit). God then has every right to command us to act holy.

A Closer Look—1 Peter 1:13–16

Let's focus in this study on 1 Peter 1:13–16. Beginning in 1:13 we are confronted with a series of strong commands. The word "therefore" that begins verse 13 reminds us to look at the preceding context of 1:1–12 to learn more about how to live out those commands. Before God commands us to live holy lives, he does things that empower us to live that way.

¹³Therefore,

prepare your minds for action;

be self-controlled;

set your hope fully on the grace to be given

   you when Jesus Christ is revealed.

¹⁴As obedient children,

do not conform to the evil desires you

   had when you lived in ignorance.

¹⁵But just as he who called you is holy,

so be holy in all you do;

¹⁶for

it is written: "Be holy, because I am holy."

Read 1:1–12 carefully and note everything that God has already done for you that makes it possible for you to live a pure and holy life.

- We have been chosen by God (v. 2).
- We have been born to a living hope (v. 3).
-
-
-
-

As you read what immediately comes after 1:13–16, you will notice that Scripture emphasizes again God's greatness (italicized) and goodness (underlined). We can't get away from God's holy love.

Other Kinds of Purity?
On the topic of purity, many people quickly think of the need for sexual purity, and rightly so. But we are called to "be holy in all [we] do." In what other areas of life is purity an urgent need?

¹⁷Since you call on <u>a Father</u> *who judges each man's work impartially, live your lives as strangers here in reverent fear.* ¹⁸For you know that it was <u>not with perishable things such as silver or gold</u> <u>that you were redeemed from the empty way of life handed down</u> <u>to you from your forefathers,</u> ¹⁹<u>but with the precious blood of Christ,</u> a lamb without blemish or defect.

The Temple

Or do you not know that your body is a temple of the Holy Spirit who is in you, whom you have from God, and that you are not your own? For you have been bought with a price: therefore glorify God in your body.

—1 Corinthians 6:19–20 NASB

Look again at 1 Peter 1:13–16 and observe any commands, comparisons, explanations, motivations, time references, and so on. Write what you see beside the passage on page 59.

What are your three most significant observations?

-
-
-

That tiny phrase "in all you do" stands tall. It refers not just to our behavior in religious settings, but to our whole way of life (Gal. 1:13; Eph. 4:22; Heb. 13:7; 1 Peter 1:18). Rather than holiness pulling us completely out of our society to hide in some "sacred" bubble, God commands us to be holy (closely connected to God) in all we do. We are to be holy in public and private, when we're working or playing, alone or in groups, on Sundays as well as Saturday nights. God calls us to be holy 24/7.

Crossing the Bridge

From your reading of the context and study of the passage, do you see any differences between Peter's original audience and us?

What are the timeless theological principles in 1 Peter 1:13–16 that connect with both the biblical audience and with us (the bridge between their town and ours)?

So What?

1. Do you think God's demand for holiness is unrealistic? Why or why not?

2. In what way has Becoming 3 helped you clarify your understanding of "holy"?

3. In what area of your life is "being holy" the most difficult struggle?

"prepare your minds for action"—This phrase literally reads "gird up the loins of your mind." In the ancient world when people needed to run fast or work hard, they had to gather up their long robes and tie them around their waist to avoid stumbling. "Mind" refers to our way of thinking or our understanding. The entire word picture reminds us that we are not playing games with God. Jesus calls us to be alert, poised for action, and focused on a single purpose.

"self-controlled"—This word means to be sober. Peter uses the same word in 4:7, where he urges us to stay sober so that we can pray, and in 5:8, where we are to be sober so that Satan won't defeat us. We automatically take this command as figurative (NASB even adds "in spirit" in 1:13; cf. 4:7; 5:8), but what Peter says in 4:1–3 and what Paul says in 1 Thessalonians 5:6–8 makes us think again.

"do not conform"—This word is found only one other place in the New Testament—Romans 12:2. The word carries the idea of being squeezed or forced into a mold. Before we came to Christ, we were shaped and molded by selfish desires for wealth, power, and pleasure. Peter warns us not to allow those former desires to control our lives now that we are Christians.

Cross-References

Lev. 11:44–45; 19:2; 20:7; Rom. 12:1–2; 1 Cor. 6:12–20; 1 Thess. 3:12–13; 4:3–8; 5:4–11; 1 Tim. 4:12; 2 Tim. 1:8–9; 2:20–21; Heb. 12:4–29; James 4:7–10; 1 Peter 2:9–12; 3:1–4; 4:1–3; 2 Peter 3:11–14; 1 John 1:5–10; 3:2–3

For Deeper Study

Arterburn, Stephen, and Fred Stoeker. *Every Man's Battle.* Colorado Springs: Water-Brook, 2000.

Bell, Rob. *Sex God: Exploring the Endless Connections Between Sexuality and Spirituality.* Grand Rapids: Zondervan, 2007.

Laaser, Mark. *Sexual Integrity in a Fallen World.* Grand Rapids: Zondervan, 1996.

Marshall, I. Howard. *1 Peter.* IVP New Testament Commentary. Downers Grove, IL: InterVarsity Press, 1991.

Winter, Lauren. *Real Sex: The Naked Truth About Chastity.* Grand Rapids: Brazos, 2005.

4. How do you usually react when you fail to act holy? How does God want you to respond to your own failure?

5. What practical steps can you take to guard yourself against falling into your "favorite" sin?

6. What more should the church do to help individual Christians live pure and holy lives?

The Weight of Glory

Humanity

So far in our journey through this workbook, we have looked at the Bible as God's inspired Word, our need to study the Bible, and the resulting virtues of truth telling and truth living. Next, we explored the mysterious but amazing conviction that God is Trinity—Father, Son, and Spirit living in an eternal relationship of self-giving love. When we accept God's offer to join his community or fellowship, we begin to allow his love to define our lives. We continued our journey by thinking about God as both good and great, a conviction that calls for a response of authentic worship—a practice that cultivates in us the quality of holiness or purity. The next page in God's grand story moves the focus from God himself to his most precious creation—human beings. Because we have been created in the image of God, we bear an enormous "weight of glory" as C. S. Lewis explains:

> It may be possible for each to think too much of his own potential glory hereafter; it is hardly possible for him to think too often or too deeply about that of his neighbour. The load, or weight, or burden of my neighbour's glory should be laid on my back, a load so heavy that only humility can carry it, and the backs of the proud will be broken. It is a serious thing to live in a society of possible gods and goddesses, to remember that the dullest and most uninteresting person you can talk to may one day be a creature which, if you saw it now, you would be strongly tempted to worship, or else a horror and a corruption such as you now meet, if at all, only in a nightmare. All day long we are, in some degree, helping each other to one or other of these destinations. . . . There are no *ordinary* people. You have never talked to a mere mortal. Nations, cultures, arts, civilizations—these are mortal, and their life is to ours as the life of a gnat. But it is immortals whom we joke with, work with, marry, snub and exploit—immortal horrors or everlasting splendours. (*The Weight of Glory*, 45–46)

The "weight" or "burden" of glory is Lewis's memorable way of describing the biblical conviction that human beings have been created in the image of God.

"image and likeness"—Older biblical scholarship believed that "image" and "likeness" were different. They claimed that "image" referred to the characteristics of personhood that remained after Adam and Eve sinned, while the "likeness" was destroyed by sin. Recent (and better) biblical scholarship says that these two parallel words are communicating a single idea—humans bear God's stamp. We were created with some capacity to mirror God, to be and act like him. We were made in his image or likeness.

Made in God's Image

Although there are only a few Scriptures that assert that we have been created in God's image, they are crystal clear and powerful.

> When God created man, he made him in the likeness of God. He created them male and female and blessed them. And when they were created, he called them "man." (Gen. 5:1b–2)

> Whoever sheds the blood of man, by man shall his blood be shed; for in the image of God has God made man. (Gen. 9:6)

> With the tongue we praise our Lord and Father, and with it we curse men, who have been made in God's likeness. Out of the same mouth come praise and cursing. My brothers, this should not be. (James 3:9–10)

A Closer Look—Genesis 1:26–28

To these three we add our focal passage for this study:

> [26]Then God said, "Let us make man in our *image*, in our *likeness*, and let them rule over the fish of the sea and the birds of the air, over the livestock, over all the earth, and over all the creatures that move along the ground."
>
> [27]So God created man in his own *image*,
>
> in the *image* of God he created him;
>
> male and female he created them.
>
> [28]God blessed them and said to them, "Be fruitful and increase in number; fill the earth and subdue it. Rule over the fish of the sea and the birds of the air and over every living creature that moves on the ground."

BELIEVING 4—*Humanity*

The three image-of-God passages in Genesis occur at very significant points in the story.

- Genesis 1—the high point of creation;
- Genesis 5—the new start following Adam and Eve's fall into sin;
- Genesis 9—the new beginning after the judgment of the flood.

These locations tell us that the "image of God" is crucial to God's plan and vital for us to understand. Since the Bible never explicitly tells us what the "image" is, there have been many attempts to define the "image" (too many to list here). Rather than trying to define what the image is, we are better off looking at what the image involves. For example, what privileges or responsibilities does it carry? As humans made in God's image, what are we supposed to do or not do? Use the questions below to help you get a better feel for what the image of God involves.

1. What does Genesis 1:26–28 suggest that the image of God involves?

2. What do you learn about the image of God from the surrounding context (Genesis 1–2)?

3. As you look at Genesis 5 and 9 and James 3, what do you learn about the image of God?

Crossing the Bridge

Remember, we cross the bridge from the ancient world to our world by identifying timeless theological truths that God is communicating. Here are a few principles related to the image of God. Be careful; taking these truths seriously will radically change your life.

- *All human beings (not just Christians) have value and dignity.* We are important because of who we are (created as important by God). We are not the mere products of naturalistic evolution. People deserve respect, and human life should be regarded as sacred.

> **Not Worthless, Only Lost**
>
> G. K. Chesterton somewhere says that the hardest thing to accept in the Christian religion is the great value it places upon the individual soul. Still older Christian writers used to say that God has hidden the majesty of the human soul from us to prevent our being ruined by vanity. This explains why even in its ruined [or sinful] condition a human being is regarded by God as something immensely worth saving. Sin does not make it worthless, but only lost.
>
> —Dallas Willard,
> *Renovation of the Heart,* 46

- *We belong to God.* We are not our own. We need God and will only find our ultimate fulfillment in God. We were meant to be God's, not gods.

- *We were created for relationships and community.* If we have been created in the image of the triune God who enjoys an eternal fellowship of love, then we too need relationships—with God and other human beings.

- *We have been granted both freedom and responsibility.* We are charged with "ruling" and "subduing" creation (Gen. 1:28). We are free to make real choices that affect the direction and destiny of our lives and others' lives. God intends for us to cooperate with him in faithfully managing creation.

- *We have been created male and female.* In an age of gender confusion, we need to know how important gender clarity is to God. We are created to live as either male or female and to interact with the other gender in a complementary partnership.

- *Sin may distort the image, but it does not destroy it.* Even after human beings chose to sin, they were told not to kill (Gen. 9) or curse (James 3) people because they have been made in God's image.

- *The image of God is perfectly manifested in Jesus Christ.*

  The god of this age has blinded the minds of unbelievers, so that they cannot see the light of the gospel of the glory of Christ, who is the image of God. (2 Cor. 4:4)

  He is the image of the invisible God. (Col. 1:15)

  The Son is the radiance of God's glory and the exact representation of his being. (Heb. 1:3)

- *Christ followers are renewed in the image of God.* As a result of our relationship with Jesus Christ, the image of God given at creation is being renewed and restored in us.

  For those God foreknew he also predestined to be conformed to the likeness of his Son, that he might be the firstborn among many brothers. (Rom. 8:29)

  And we, who with unveiled faces all reflect the Lord's glory, are being transformed into his likeness with ever-increasing glory, which comes from the Lord, who is the Spirit. (2 Cor. 3:18)

  You were taught, with regard to your former way of life, to put off your old self, which is being corrupted by its deceitful desires; to be made new in the attitude of your minds; and to put on the new self, created to be like God in true righteousness and holiness. (Eph. 4:22–24)

Do not lie to each other, since you have taken off your old self with its practices and have put on the new self, which is being renewed in knowledge in the image of its Creator. (Col. 3:9–10)

When God created us in his image, he gave us dignity and value, entrusted us with significant freedom and responsibility, and gave us the privilege of relating to him. In Christ, the image of God is being restored in us. In sum, in Christ we are becoming fully human!

Brennan Manning tells a story about Ed Farrell, who traveled from his home in the United States to spend two weeks with his uncle, who lived in Ireland. His uncle was celebrating his eightieth birthday. Early on the morning of his birthday, Ed and his uncle took a walk along the shore of Lake Killarney, enjoying the beautiful scenery. For twenty minutes they walked in silence, captivated by the moment. Then his uncle began to do a strange thing for an eighty-year-old man—he began to skip along the shore like a young boy. When Ed caught up with him, he asked, "Uncle Seamus, you look very happy. Do you want to tell me why?" "Yes," said the old man, his face covered in tears. "You see, the Father is very fond of me. Ah, me Father is so very fond of me" (Manning, *Wisdom of Tenderness*, 25–26). Do you get it? The God who created you in his image is very fond of you!

So What?

1. Describe what you assume God thinks or feels when he thinks about you.

2. Is there anything that keeps you from realizing (with both your mind and your heart) that the Father is very fond of you?

Cross-References

Look back over the references cited throughout Believing 4.

For Deeper Study

Gushee, David P. *Only Human*. San Francisco: Jossey-Bass, 2005.

Lewis, C. S., *The Weight of Glory*. 1949. San Francisco: HarperSanFranciso, 1980.

Sherlock, Charles. *The Doctrine of Humanity*. Downers Grove, IL: InterVarsity Press, 1996.

Walton, John H. *Genesis*. NIV Application Commentary. Grand Rapids: Zondervan, 2001.

Wilkins, Michael J. *In His Image: Reflecting Christ in Everyday Life*. Colorado Springs: NavPress, 1997.

Willard, Dallas. *Renovation of the Heart*. Colorado Springs: NavPress, 2002.

3. Does your primary identity in life come from God's estimation of you or from another source? Explain.

4. Acknowledging our humanity means accepting God's love, admitting that we have limits, cultivating godly relationships, learning how to use freedom, taking responsibility and developing a healthy understanding of human sexuality, just to name a few things. In what way is the Spirit leading you to acknowledge your humanity right now in your life?

5. What can we do as a community of Christ followers to remind each other of how important we are to God?

What on Earth Are We Here For?

Seeking the Kingdom

Because God created us in his image, we are loaded with value and importance. We are free to choose but entrusted with responsibility. We are male or female. We were created to live in community. We belong to God and need God in order to be fully alive human beings. God's original plan for creating us in his image can be fulfilled only in Jesus Christ, who is able to restore the image of God in us.

This glory of being created in God's image carries enormous weight. (Life is tough when you're important!) Some people can't handle the significance of being a valuable human being, so they squander the blessing. In other words, they forget about God and pursue their own selfish agendas. In Behaving 4 Jesus tells us how to make the most of being an image bearer by seeking God and his purposes for our lives. Because we have been created in God's image, we have important work to do—kingdom work.

Although not flashy or famous, Rick Warren's father faithfully imaged his heavenly Father.

My father was a minister for over fifty years, serving mostly in small, rural churches. He was a simple preacher, but he was a man with a mission. His favorite activity was taking teams of volunteers overseas to build church buildings for small congregations. In his lifetime, Dad built over 150 churches around the world.

In 1999, my father died of cancer. In the final week of his life the disease kept him awake in a semi-conscious state nearly twenty-four hours a day. As he dreamed, he'd talk out loud about what he was dreaming. Sitting by his bedside, I learned a lot about my dad by just listening to his dreams. He relived one church building project after another.

"first"—This refers to what is of first importance (i.e., "above all else"), rather than first in time, like the first item on a long list of equally important items. God's kingdom and righteousness are on a list by themselves.

"kingdom"—God's rule or reign that is present now in Jesus Christ (and those who belong to him) and will be fully realized when Christ returns to establish his eternal kingdom.

"righteousness"—Right relationship with God that comes through Christ's saving work, as well as the godly conduct and behavior that comes as the only right response to God's gracious work.

Do What You Are

Usually when we meet someone for the first time, it isn't long before we ask, "What do you do?" . . . Work takes up so many of our waking hours that our jobs come to define us and give us our identities. We become what we do.

Calling reverses such thinking. A sense of calling should precede a choice of job and career, and the main way to discover calling is along the line of what we are each created and gifted to be. Instead of "You are what you do," calling says, "Do what you are."

—Os Guinness, *The Call*, 46

One night near the end, while my wife, my niece, and I were by his side, Dad suddenly became very active and tried to get out of bed. Of course, he was too weak, and my wife insisted he lay back down. But he persisted in trying to get out of bed, so my wife finally asked, "Jimmy, what are you trying to do?" He replied, "Got to save one more for Jesus! Got to save one more for Jesus! Got to save one more for Jesus!" He began to repeat that phrase over and over.

During the next hour, he said the phrase probably a hundred times. "Got to save one more for Jesus!" As I sat by his bed with tears flowing down my cheeks, I bowed my head to thank God for my dad's faith. At that moment Dad reached out and placed his frail hand on my head and said, as if commissioning me, "Save one more for Jesus! Save one more for Jesus!" (*Purpose-Driven Life*, 287).

Jimmy Warren was a man who knew God's purpose for his life and embraced it fully.

Career or Calling?

In his book *The Will of God as a Way of Life,* Jerry Sittser defines a *career* as a particular line of work that requires education or training, earns an income, and keeps our society running. A *calling*, on the other hand, is a person's specific, God-given purpose for living. Our calling refers to the way God wants us to use our time, energy, resources, and abilities to carry out his purposes in this world. Rick Warren's father used his career as a small-church pastor to carry out his life calling of leading people to faith in Christ. Here are some other ways to use a career to live out a life calling (see *Will of God*, 165–68):

- "Managing a sporting goods store is a career; challenging people to use their leisure time to find refreshment and renewal is a calling."
- "Teaching social studies at a junior high is a career; providing instruction, support, and guidance to adolescents going through a difficult passage in life is a calling."
- "Functioning as a secretary is a career; organizing an office so that details are handled efficiently, but never at the expense of people, is a calling."

The primary calling of every believer is to trust and obey Jesus Christ, but God seems to call individual believers to specific responsibilities in his kingdom. Our individual calling will grow out of our gifts, abilities, personality, and life experiences. Too often we confuse career and calling, but they are not the same. Our calling is much more important.

A career causes people to think of income, power, position, and prestige. A calling inspires people to consider human need, moral standards, and a larger perspective. A career does not define a person, nor does it determine a calling. If anything, the opposite occurs. God defines the person and gives that person a calling. Then he or she is free to use a career for God's kingdom purpose. (Sittser, *Will of God*, 166)

A Closer Look—Matthew 6:33

The belief that God is our Creator and we are creatures made in his image leads to the habit of seeking him and his purposes as our highest ambition in life. When we talk about life purpose, we are talking much more about calling than career. Jesus gets to the point in Matthew 6:33.

But

seek first his kingdom and his righteousness,

and

all these things will be given to you as well.

1. Take a moment and look carefully at this verse, noting any contrasts, commands, important pronouns, promises, and so on. Mark your observations in the space above.

2. What is the major theme of the section that contains 6:33?

3. The word "but" that begins verse 33 signals a contrast between seeking God's kingdom and what?

4. What does the phrase "all these things" refer back to?

Crossing the Bridge

In this passage, what are the differences between the biblical audience and us?

Jesus commands us to turn our backs on the god Possession and to turn our primary attention to the quest for the Father's royalty and righteousness. This is not a counsel to seek "spiritual" things instead of material things, or inward things instead of outward things; it is counsel to seek God's things rather than our own. . . . Jesus creates higher loves in us in order to drive out the lower loves.

—F. D. Bruner, *Christbook*, 268

"All These Things"?
What happens when God's promise to meet the basic needs of Christians seems to go unfulfilled and his people experience starvation? One possible solution is that God expects to fulfill this promise through his people.

When God's people corporately seek first his priorities, they will by definition take care of the needy in their fellowships. When one considers that over 50 percent of all believers now live in the Two-Thirds World and that a substantial majority of those believers live below what we would consider the poverty line, a huge challenge to First-World Christians emerges. Without a doubt, most individual and church budgets need drastic realignment in terms of what Christians spend on themselves versus what they spend on others.

—Craig Blomberg, *Matthew*, 126–27

Cross-References
Ps. 37; Matt. 6:9–13; 7:24–27; Luke 12:13–34; 16:19–31; 1 Cor. 15:58; Col. 3:23; 1 Tim. 6:17–19

For Deeper Study
Guinness, Os. *The Call: Finding and Fulfilling the Central Purpose of Your Life.* Nashville: Word, 1998.

Packer, J. I. *God's Plans for You.* Wheaton, IL: Crossway, 2001.

Sittser, Gerald L. *The Will of God as a Way of Life: Finding and Following the Will of God.* Grand Rapids: Zondervan, 2000.

Warren, Rick. *The Purpose-Driven Life.* Grand Rapids: Zondervan, 2002.

As you cross from the ancient world to our world, what are the timeless theological truths that Jesus is communicating in Matthew 6:33?

So What?

1. What does being created in the image of God (Gen. 1:26–28) have to do with seeking first God's kingdom and righteousness (Matt. 6:33)?

2. What is your controlling drive, your ultimate quest, your greatest passion? What do you spend most of your time and energy seeking?

3. In one or two sentences write out your life calling. Why has God put you on this earth?

4. What are some careers that could help you fulfill your life calling?

5. Is it necessary to have a career related to your calling?

Come to Me,
All Who Are Weary

Rest

Yes, we've been created in the image of God and called to seek his kingdom. God says, "You're important and I have something important for you to do." We have been hardwired for abounding in "the work of the Lord" (1 Cor. 15:58). Deep down we want to live out God's calling with passion and fervor. We want to pursue our kingdom assignment with a radical devotion and wholehearted abandonment, pouring out our lives as an offering to the Lord. We want to do all that, but we're weak and sinful human beings who lose focus and lose sleep and sometimes spin ourselves into a chronic state of exhaustion and discouragement. There should be a partnership between zealous work and intentional rest (John 15). To glorify God we must not only work with all our hearts, but also learn to rest for the sake of our souls. In Becoming 4, we will learn about the much-needed (but often neglected) character quality of rest.

Take a moment and read Matthew 11:20–24 and 12:1–14 (skip over 11:25–30 for now). What do these two sections have in common (hint: a certain response to Jesus)?

36 Life Essentials

BELIEVING
Authority of the Bible
Triune God
Great and Good God
Humanity
Satan and Sin
Jesus Christ
Salvation
Holy Spirit
The Church
Transformation
Mission
The End

BEHAVING
Studying the Bible
Fellowshiping
Worshiping
Seeking the Kingdom
Waging Spiritual War
Following
Trusting and Acting
Walking by the Spirit
Serving
Praying
Engaging the World
Persevering

BECOMING
Truth
Love
Purity
➤ **Rest**
Freedom
New Identity in Christ
Assurance
Fruit of the Spirit
Humility
Peace
Compassion
Hope

73

"weary"—This word is often translated "labor" or "work" (see Luke 5:5; Acts 20:35; Rom. 16:6, 12; 1 Cor. 4:12; 1 Tim. 4:10; 5:17). Sometimes the word refers to being "tired" or "weary" from hard work, and that is likely what it means in this context (cf. Rev. 2:3). Jesus invites those who are fatigued and exhausted to come to him for rest.

"burdened"—This term describes a physical or emotional/spiritual load or burden. In Acts 27:10 the noun form refers to a ship's cargo. In Matthew 23:4 and Luke 11:46 Jesus rebukes

SCRIPTURE NOTES

the scribes and Pharisees for loading down people with unrealistic religious burdens. Jesus invites those who are overwhelmed and weighed down to come to him for rest.

"yoke"—Literally, the word refers to a wooden frame used to join two animals so that they can pull heavy loads. Figuratively, "yoke" symbolizes a person's submission to an authority. The Jews often used "yoke" to refer to the Law. In contrast, Jesus' yoke is his teaching, since we learn from him by submitting to his teaching. Jesus doesn't command us to take on the burden of religious externalism, nor does he say, "Do as you please." While we may think that what tired people need most is a vacation, Jesus offers them an even more restful gift—a whole new way of doing life.

Now read Matthew 11:25–30. How does this section differ from the two surrounding sections (hint: a certain response to Jesus)?

In 11:25–30 we see that it is not the "important" people who respond positively to Jesus but the little children and the weary and burdened. For those who submit to his "yoke," Jesus offers "rest." Let's take a closer look at Matthew 11:28–30.

A Closer Look—Matthew 11:28–30

²⁸Come to me, all you who are weary and burdened,

and I will give you rest.

²⁹Take my yoke upon you and learn from me,

for I am gentle and humble in heart,

and you will find rest for your souls.

³⁰For my yoke is easy and my burden is light.

1. What are the three commands in this passage?

2. What is the tone of these three commands?

3. What kind of people are invited to carry out these commands?

4. What promises are attached to the commands?

5. Circle every reference to Jesus ("I," "me," "my") in the passage on page 74. Why is it so important that Jesus gives personal commands (e.g., "Come to *me*")?

6. As you read the passage carefully, what other significant things do you see?

The most explicit promise in this passage is that those who come to Jesus will find rest. What does this mean? The New Testament speaks of *rest* in at least three different ways.

1. Physical rest

   Then, because so many people were coming and going that they did not even have a chance to eat, he said to them, "Come with me by yourselves to a quiet place and get some rest." (Mark 6:31)

2. Spiritual or relational rest

   By all this we are encouraged. In addition to our own encouragement, we were especially delighted to see how happy Titus was, because his spirit has been refreshed [given rest] by all of you. (2 Cor. 7:13)

3. Eternal rest

   There remains, then, a Sabbath-rest for the people of God; for anyone who enters God's rest also rests from his own work, just as God did from his. Let us, therefore, make every effort to enter that rest, so that no one will fall by following their example of disobedience. (Heb. 4:9–11)

Jesus invites us to come to him to experience a holistic rest that includes all of the above.

Crossing the Bridge

Although we are not usually tempted to submit to Old Testament Law, are we sometimes "wearied" and "burdened" by religious regulations forced on us from the outside? Can you think of examples in your life?

Jesus invites people who are overwhelmed (by life, religion, etc.) to come to him and take his burden upon them. The scribes and Pharisees of Jesus' day were putting heavy burdens on people. In Luke 11:46 Jesus says, "And you experts in the law, woe to you, because you load people down with burdens they can hardly carry, and you yourselves will not lift one finger to help them." Yet we know that the "yoke" is a symbol of work and authority, not of ease and lawlessness. We need to be reminded that "Jesus' yoke is not lighter because he demands less, but because he bears more of the load with the burdened" (Keener, *Matthew*, 349). Jesus offers work that is refreshing and good because the Holy Spirit gives strength. Following Jesus means a whole new way of living and bearing responsibilities. He is our gentle and humble teacher who leads by example (cf. Phil. 2).

What other theological principles do you see in Matthew 11:28–30?

So What?

1. How does physical rest relate to emotional and spiritual rest?

2. How would you say you are doing when it comes to balancing "abounding" (working) and "abiding" (resting)?

3. Why does our culture seem to place more value on abounding than on abiding?

4. What do you do to experience rest and renewal? Do these activities deliver real rest, or do they actually drain you even more?

5. What is the difference between (1) taking some time off from school or work and (2) discovering a whole new way of bearing responsibilities?

6. Living overloaded lives means that we fail to acknowledge our limits. What keeps you from acknowledging your limits?

7. What is your best advice for people who have a hard time saying no to more responsibilities and commitments?

Cross-References
Gen. 2:3; Exod. 23:12; 33:14; Ps. 116:7; Jer. 6:16; Acts 15:10; Gal. 5:1; Heb. 4:1–13; 1 John 5:3; Rev. 14:13

For Deeper Study
Buchanan, Mark. *The Rest of God: Restoring Your Soul by Restoring Sabbath*. Nashville: W Publishing Group, 2006.

Hughes, Kent R. *Liberating Ministry from the Success Syndrome*. Wheaton, IL: Crossway, 2008.

Kuhatschek, Jack. *The Superman Syndrome*. Grand Rapids: Zondervan, 1995.

Swenson, Richard A. *Margin*. Colorado Springs: NavPress, 1992.

Webster, Doug. *The Easy Yoke*. Colorado Springs: NavPress, 1995.

Not the Way It's Supposed to Be

Satan and Sin

Once, when I was in college, a senior adult from our church invited me and several of my friends to eat Sunday dinner at her house. This godly matriarch of our country congregation also happened to be the personification of Southern sophistication. When we arrived at her home, the formal dining-room table was set with china, silver, and crystal. We could see the roast and gravy, the mashed potatoes supporting tiny lakes of butter, the carefully seasoned garden vegetables, and the homemade rolls. We guessed that there had to be a bodacious dessert hiding close by. Soon after we started devouring the delicious meal, I used a small silver spoon to scoop white powder from a crystal cube into my iced tea. "Several scoops of sugar ought to do it," I reasoned. When I took a big drink of my "sweet" tea, it didn't taste like sweet tea. It didn't even taste like unsweetened tea; it tasted like the ocean. Something had gone terribly wrong. To make a long story short, I had liberally salted my iced tea.

The story of Scripture takes a similar, but much more serious turn in Genesis 3. As you read the first two chapters of Genesis, you can't help but notice the repeated phrase, "God saw that it was good." All is well with God's creation. God even gives Eve to Adam as the perfect partner, and together they experience an intimate relationship with God and harmony with his creation. Then something goes terribly wrong, something much worse than pouring salt into a glass of iced tea. In Genesis 3 the background music changes as the deceiver crawls onto the scene and tempts Eve and Adam to take matters into their own hands (sin). They believe the lies of the serpent and act upon them. The results of their sin are disastrous, for both them and their descendants. We continue to suffer the consequences even today.

The Shattering of Shalom

The story of Scripture begins with our great and good God creating human beings in his image. Our triune God is the perfect community and created us to experience that life-giving community. A good biblical word for God's original plan for wholeness, delight, and abundance is the Hebrew word *shalom* ("peace"). This word refers to the "way things ought to be" as God, humans, and all creation live together in a perfect world.

The story takes a dark and dreadful turn in Genesis 3, however, when Satan and sin spoil God's good creation. More than anything, sin is the purposeful breaking of shalom. God hates sin "because it interferes with the way things are supposed to be" (Plantinga, *Not the Way It's Supposed to Be*, 14). As much as we would like to ignore this part of the story, we must face it in order to see how God wants to bring about a happy ending to the story by restoring the shalom he originally intended.

A Closer Look—Genesis 3:1–7

[1]Now the serpent was more crafty than any of the wild animals

the LORD God had made. He said to the woman, "Did God

really say, 'You must not eat from any tree in the garden'?"

Although the Genesis story never specifically identifies the serpent as Satan or the Devil, this is the clear teaching of the New Testament:

> You belong to your father, the devil, and you want to carry out your father's desire. He was a murderer from the beginning, not holding to the truth, for there is no truth in him. When he lies, he speaks his native language, for he is a liar and the father of lies. (John 8:44)

> The great dragon was hurled down—that ancient serpent called the devil, or Satan, who leads the whole world astray. (Rev. 12:9)

> He seized the dragon, that ancient serpent, who is the devil, or Satan, and bound him for a thousand years. (Rev. 20:2)

1. Satan (meaning "adversary" or "opponent") is the chief evil spirit in a kingdom of evil. Look up the following verses, and write down what they say about Satan and his work.

   • Matthew 4:1–11

   • Mark 4:13–20

"crafty"—The serpent is described as "crafty," that is, "shrewd" or "cunning." The word itself is neutral and can carry either a positive or a negative meaning. In Proverbs 1:4; 8:5; and 15:5, the Hebrew word is translated "prudence" by the NIV and is considered a virtue. In Genesis 3 and at other places in the Old Testament (Exod. 21:14; Job 5:12; 15:5) the word carries a negative sense of evil plotting and scheming.

SCRIPTURE NOTES

Do We Trust God?

The beginning of all sin—the origin of all that is unloving—is a judgment about God. We embrace a picture of God that is less loving, less beautiful, less full of life, less gracious, and less glorious than the true God really is. . . . When our picture of God is distorted, we can no longer trust God to be the source of our life. . . . If the deceiving Accuser is successful in distorting our mental picture of God so that God appears incapable or unwilling to give us life, we invariably look elsewhere to find life.

—Gregory Boyd,
Repenting of Religion, 127–28

What Exactly Is Sin?

There are more than thirty words in the New Testament alone that convey the idea of sin. One reliable theologian defines sin as "any act, attitude, or disposition which fails to completely fulfill or measure up to the standards of God's righteousness. It may involve an actual transgression of God's law or failure to live up to his norms" (Erickson, *Concise Dictionary*, 152).

When we disobey or rebel, we sin. When we fall short of God's standard, we sin. When we place something other than God in God's place, we sin. When we listen to impressions rather than God's instructions, we sin. When we pervert God's good gifts into something self-serving, we sin. When we refuse to admit that we are needy creatures, we sin. We have all sinned and failed to live up to God's glorious design. And sin pays a wage—death.

- Mark 5:1–20

- John 12:30–32

- 2 Corinthians 4:4

- 2 Corinthians 11:14

- Ephesians 4:27

- Ephesians 6:11

- Hebrews 2:14–15

- James 4:7

- 1 Peter 5:8

- 1 John 3:8–10

- Revelation 12:7–9

2. In Genesis 3 Satan's strategy to deceive Eve begins with a loaded question. What is the deceiver trying to accomplish by starting the temptation in this way? What do you see imbedded in the serpent's question?

SCRIPTURE NOTES

²The woman said to the serpent, "We may eat fruit from the trees in the garden, ³but God did say, 'You must not eat fruit from the tree that is in the middle of the garden, and you must not touch it, or you will die.'"

3. When Eve corrects the serpent, she actually goes too far and puts words in God's mouth. Carefully compare God's instructions in Genesis 2:16–17 with Eve's paraphrase in 3:2–3. What does Eve add?

God's Love Comes First

But God demonstrates his own love for us in this: While we were still sinners, Christ died for us.

—Romans 5:8

SCRIPTURE NOTES

4"You will not surely die," the serpent said to the woman. 5"For

God knows that when you eat of it your eyes will be opened,

and you will be like God, knowing good and evil."

4. These verses reveal the next phase in the serpent's strategy. What does this involve?

SCRIPTURE NOTES

6When the woman saw that the fruit of the tree was good for

food and pleasing to the eye, and also desirable for gaining

wisdom, she took some and ate it. She also gave some to her

husband, who was with her, and he ate it.

5. Look at the verbs in verse 6 and identify the specific steps to sin.

⁷Then the eyes of both of them were opened, and they realized they were naked; so they sewed fig leaves together and made coverings for themselves.

Take and Eat

She took . . . and ate—so simple the act, so hard its undoing. God will taste poverty and death before "take and eat" become verbs of salvation.

—Derek Kidner, *Genesis*, 68

Evil in Disguise

Satan must appeal to our God-given appetite for goodness in order to win his way. . . . To prevail, evil must leech not only power and intelligence from goodness but also its credibility. From counterfeit money to phony airliner parts to the trustworthy look on the face of a con artist, evil appears in disguise. Hence its treacherousness. Hence the need for the Holy Spirit's gift of discernment. Hence the sheer difficulty, at times, of distinguishing what is good from what is evil.

—Cornelius Plantinga,
Not the Way It's Supposed to Be, 98

6. We have now moved from temptation to sin to consequences. Read the rest of Genesis 3 and record how sin affects relationships:

   • Effects on the sinner's relationship with God

   • Effects on the sinner

   • Effects on the sinner's relationships with other humans

Crossing the Bridge

In order to cross the bridge from the ancient world to our world, we need to identify timeless theological truths that God is trying to teach us. There are a few principles listed below. What other theological principles do you see in Genesis 3:1–7?

   • The tempter does not give up easily. Even after Eve's initial resistance, he keeps on pressuring her to sin.

   • The tempter twists and distorts God's Word.

   •

   •

   •

   •

So What?

1. In the sinless garden environment, Adam and Eve still have God-given limits (2:16–17). What does that arrangement say about the nature of true freedom?

BELIEVING 5—*Satan and Sin*

2. Satan's strategy to tempt human beings is subtle, deceitful, and complex. What aspect of that ancient strategy do you struggle with the most (e.g., not knowing what God really said, doubting God's motives)?

3. How does understanding Satan's strategy help us better understand the nature of sin?

4. C. S. Lewis once wrote, "There are two equal and opposite errors into which our [human] race can fall about the devils. One is to disbelieve in their existence. The other is to believe, and to feel an excessive and unhealthy interest in them. They themselves are equally pleased by both errors" (*Screwtape Letters*, ix). Do you tend toward one extreme or the other? What do you need in order to be more discerning?

5. When is it most difficult to trust that God wants what is best for you?

6. How do you see people acting as if they were God? What is your greatest struggle in this area?

Cross-References
See the earlier references to Satan along with the following references to sin: Ps. 51; Matt. 4:1–11; Rom. 1–3; 5:6–8; 6:23; 8:1–4; 2 Cor. 11:14–15; Eph. 2:1–6; James 1:13–15; 4:17; 1 John 1:8–10; 2:15–17

For Deeper Study
Lewis, C. S. *The Screwtape Letters*. New York: Macmillan, 1961.
Plantinga, Cornelius. *Not the Way It's Supposed to Be: A Breviary of Sin*. Grand Rapids: Eerdmans, 1995.
Walton, John H. *Genesis*. NIV Application Commentary. Grand Rapids: Zondervan, 2001.

Our Struggle Is Not Against Flesh and Blood

Waging Spiritual War

We don't live in a perfect world. We have enemies. Satan entices us to look for life apart from God, and sometimes we take him up on the offer. The consequences can be deadly. The apostle Peter tells us that our "enemy the devil prowls around like a roaring lion looking for someone to devour" (1 Peter 5:8). We also battle our own sinful tendency to walk away from God, to go our own way. We read in Romans that "all have sinned and fall short of the glory of God" (3:23), and we can relate. Yes, we have enemies, but we also have a Savior who has conquered those enemies. In Jesus' showdown with Satan at the beginning of our Lord's public ministry, he doesn't retreat in ignorance or cower in fear. Instead Jesus wins the victory in the Judean wilderness and advances the kingdom of God. In Behaving 5, we look to Jesus' example of how to wage spiritual war. Get ready to put on your armor!

In his profoundly insightful and inspiring book, *The Jesus I Never Knew*, Philip Yancey observes how Jesus' temptation in the wilderness reveals the difference between how God works and how Satan works and teaches us that goodness cannot be imposed from the outside; it must grow from the inside out.

The Temptation in the desert reveals a profound difference between God's power and Satan's power. Satan has the power to coerce, to dazzle, to force obedience, to destroy. Humans have learned much from that power, and governments draw deeply from its reservoir. With a bullwhip or a billy club or an AK-47, human beings can force other human beings to do just about anything they want. . . . Satan's power is external and coercive.

God's power, in contrast, is internal and noncoercive. . . . Such power may seem at times like weakness. In its commitment to transform gently from the inside out and in its relentless dependence on human choice, God's power may resemble a kind of abdication. As every parent and every lover knows, love can be rendered powerless if the beloved chooses to spurn it. . . .

Although power can force obedience, only love can summon a response of love, which is the one thing God wants from us and the reason he created us. . . . Love has its own power, the only power ultimately capable of conquering the human heart. (pages 76–78)

Part of waging spiritual war includes understanding your enemy. Satan tries to coerce, to force, to overpower, but how? What is his strategy? Adam and Eve's experience in the garden (Gen. 3) and Jesus' battle in the desert (Matt. 4) answer that question.

A Closer Look—Matthew 4:1–11

Take a moment and read Matthew 3:13–4:17. Notice anything in these surrounding paragraphs that might help you understand 4:1–11. For example, you might notice that Jesus had just heard his Father say, "This is My Son" (3:17) before going into the desert to hear Satan say, "If [Since] you are the Son . . ." This tells us that Satan is not really doubting that Jesus is the Son of God. Rather, he is tempting Jesus to use his divine power in selfish ways.

1. What else do you see in the surrounding context of 3:13–17 and 4:12–17?

Now look carefully at the passage itself. Note repeated words or phrases, commands, contrasts, purpose statements, time and place references, and so on. Mark up the passage below and make comments in the margins.

¹Then Jesus was led by the Spirit into the desert to be tempted

by the devil. ²After fasting forty days and forty nights, he was

hungry. ³The tempter came to him and said, "If you are the Son

"it is written"—Each time Jesus answers Satan's temptation, he answers with "it is written" followed by a quotation from his Bible, the Old Testament. All three times Jesus quotes from Deuteronomy 6–8. This part of Deuteronomy records Moses' sermons to the people of Israel just before they crossed the Jordan River into the Promised Land. Moses was challenging Israel to be faithful!

Ironically, Jesus had just been baptized in the same Jordan River and was about to begin his public ministry. Jesus, the obedient Son, came to do what the disobedient children of Israel had failed to do. When tempted to do the right thing at the wrong time, or to test God rather than trust him, or to take a shortcut to his crown, Jesus responds by citing God's Word in context.

A Mighty Fortress
And though this world, with devils filled,
Should threaten to undo us,
We will not fear, for God hath willed
His truth to triumph through us.
The Prince of Darkness grim,
We tremble not for him;
His rage we can endure,
For lo, his doom is sure,
One little word shall fell him.

—Martin Luther,
"A Mighty Fortress Is Our God"

SCRIPTURE NOTES

of God, tell these stones to become bread." ⁴Jesus answered, "It is written: 'Man does not live on bread alone, but on every word that comes from the mouth of God.'" ⁵Then the devil took him to the holy city and had him stand on the highest point of the temple. ⁶"If you are the Son of God," he said, "throw yourself down. For it is written: 'He will command his angels concerning you, and they will lift you up in their hands, so that you will not strike your foot against a stone.'" ⁷Jesus answered him, "It is also written: 'Do not put the Lord your God to the test.'" ⁸Again, the devil took him to a very high mountain and showed him all the kingdoms of the world and their splendor. ⁹"All this I will give you," he said, "if you will bow down and worship me." ¹⁰Jesus said to him, "Away from me, Satan! For it is written: 'Worship the Lord your God, and serve him only.'" ¹¹Then the devil left him, and angels came and attended him.

A Desperate Housewife
Read Genesis 39 and put yourself in Joseph's place. Reflect on the things that set him up for temptation, on his response, on the cost of resisting, and so on. What is the main thing you take away from this interesting story about waging spiritual battle?

2. Think a moment about the similarities between Satan's strategy in tempting Adam and Eve (Gen. 3:1–7) and his strategy in tempting Jesus (Matt. 4:1–11). Make a list of the tempter's strategies that are common to both situations.

- Satan raises doubts about God's Word.
- Satan appeals to their physical desires.
-
-
-
-
-
-
-
-

BEHAVING 5—*Waging Spiritual War*

Look carefully at your list since it offers a significant clue about what to expect from the tempter in your own life. His strategy doesn't change.

Crossing the Bridge

In order to cross the bridge from the ancient world to our world, we need to identify timeless theological truths that God is trying to teach us. There are a few principles listed below. What other theological principles do you see in Matthew 4:1–11?

- The same situation can be experienced by the same person as both a test from God and a temptation from Satan. Jesus was "led *by the Spirit* into the desert to be tempted *by the devil.*"

- The essence of temptation is to twist something good into something evil. Usually a temptation is not something inherently evil, but something good used for evil purposes. One very important aspect of waging spiritual war is to know the true purpose, God's purpose, for things we encounter in life.

-

-

-

-

-

So What?

1. When Satan tempts Jesus, he appeals to several universal human desires. What are they? How does Satan appeal to those same desires when tempting you?

Does the Armor Fit?

Be strong with the Lord's mighty power. Put on all of God's armor so that you will be able to stand firm against all strategies and tricks of the Devil. For we are not fighting against people made of flesh and blood, but against the evil rulers and authorities of the unseen world, against those mighty powers of darkness who rule this world, and against wicked spirits in the heavenly realms. Use every piece of God's armor to resist the enemy in the time of evil, so that after the battle you will still be standing firm. Stand your ground, putting on the sturdy belt of truth and the body armor of God's righteousness. For shoes, put on the peace that comes from the Good News, so that you will be fully prepared. In every battle you will need faith as your shield to stop the fiery arrows aimed at you by Satan. Put on salvation as your helmet, and take the sword of the Spirit, which is the word of God. Pray at all times and on every occasion in the power of the Holy Spirit. Stay alert and be persistent in your prayers for all Christians everywhere.

—Ephesians 6:10–18 NLT

Cross-References
Gen. 39; 1 Cor. 10:13; Eph. 6:10–20; Heb. 4:15–16; James 4:1–10

For Deeper Study
Arnold, Clinton. *Three Crucial Questions About Spiritual Warfare.* Grand Rapids: Baker, 1997.

Fape, Michael O. *Powers in Encounter with Power.* Scotland: Christian Focus, 2003.

Wilkins, Michael J. *Matthew.* NIV Application Commentary. Grand Rapids: Zondervan, 2004.

Wright, Nigel Goring. *A Theology of the Dark Side: Putting the Power of Evil in Its Place.* Downers Grove, IL: InterVarsity Press, 2003.

2. Since evil is usually a perverting and twisting of something good, temptation will often relate to some God-given need in our lives. What legitimate needs do you have that are not being met? How are you tempted to meet those needs in illegitimate ways?

3. One of Jesus' weapons for waging spiritual war is using Scripture. What other weapons do you see Jesus using in Matthew 4:1–11?

4. Read Ephesians 6:10–18 in the sidebar on page 87. What role should prayer play in waging spiritual war?

5. When are you most vulnerable to spiritual attack?

6. Summarize the main thing you have learned in Behaving 5 about waging spiritual war.

7. As you think about a temptation you are now facing in your life, how can you apply what you have learned to your particular situation?

Free at Last, Free at Last

Freedom

Our belief that Satan and sin are dangerous enemies leads to the practice of waging spiritual warfare. We turned to Jesus' temptations in the desert to see how he countered the lies and deception of the Evil One. Very simply, he defeated Satan by trusting his Father, relying upon the truth of the Scriptures, and walking in obedience. The character quality that results from a belief in the reality of spiritual enemies and the habit of waging war against them is freedom—the topic of Becoming 5.

On August 28, 1963, Martin Luther King Jr. stood at a podium at the Lincoln Memorial in Washington DC and delivered his famous "I Have a Dream" speech. One hundred years earlier Abraham Lincoln had signed the Emancipation Proclamation, a "momentous decree" King said, that "came as a beacon light of hope to millions of Negro slaves, . . . a joyous daybreak to the end of the long night of their captivity." King's message culminates with the following words:

And when this happens, when we allow freedom to ring, when we let it ring from every village and every hamlet, from every state and every city, we will be able to speed up that day when *all* of God's children, black men and white men, Jews and Gentiles, Protestants and Catholics, will be able to join hands and sing in the words of the old Negro spiritual,

> *"Free at last, free at last.*
> *Thank God Almighty, we are free at last."*

King was a Baptist minister whose deep Christian faith fueled his passion for leading the civil rights movement in the turbulent America of the 1960s. As a result of his courageous commitment to fight for the social

SCRIPTURE NOTES

implications of the gospel of Jesus Christ, Martin Luther King Jr. was assassinated April 4, 1968, on the balcony outside his Memphis hotel room.

The God revealed in Scripture is a God of deliverance. The Old Testament offers many examples of God setting people free. The greatest example, of course, is the exodus, when God delivered his people from slavery in Egypt. The famous Ten Commandments of Exodus 20 begin with these words—"I am the LORD your God, who brought you out of Egypt, out of the land of slavery" (v. 2). The Old Testament also looks forward to a time when God would make a new covenant with his people and write his law on their hearts (Jer. 31:33). He would set them free from the inside out through the work of his Spirit. Leading his people out of slavery in Egypt was a preview of the ultimate work of rescue and deliverance accomplished by Jesus Christ. At the cross God condemned the power of sin so that all who respond to Jesus are no longer condemned but set free to live—really live!

A Closer Look—Romans 8:1–4

1. Read Romans 7. What is Paul's dilemma in this chapter?

Now look at Romans 8:1–4 below. Read the passage carefully, marking important words, purpose statements, prepositions, explanations, conjunctions, and so on. In addition, make comments, show connections, or ask questions in the margins.

[1]Therefore, there is now no condemnation for those who are in Christ Jesus, [2]because through Christ Jesus the law of the Spirit of life set me free from the law of sin and death. [3]For what the law was powerless to do in that it was weakened by the sinful nature, God did by sending his own Son in the likeness of sinful man to be a sin offering. And so he condemned sin in sinful man, [4]in order that the righteous requirements of the law might be fully met in us, who do not live according to the sinful nature but according to the Spirit.

2. Why is there no condemnation for us? What is the absolute requirement to receive the pardon? What else does this text say about condemnation?

3. If God's law is good, why is it powerless to set us free?

4. What are the three "laws" in this text, and how do they relate to each other?

5. When it says in verse 3 that "God did" something, what did God actually do?

6. How can we meet the demands and standards of God's perfect law?

Crossing the Bridge

This passage is loaded with theological truths that can make a big difference in our lives. For example, rules (law) are good, but they have no power to set us free from sin. Rules can only show us what is right and wrong; they cannot help us do what is right or avoid what is wrong. The Law points out the problem, but it is powerless to supply a solution. What other theological principles do you see in Romans 8:1–4?

•

•

•

"condemnation"—The underlying Greek word occurs only in Romans 5:16 and 18 and here in 8:1 in the New Testament. This legal term refers to judgment against someone and the resulting penalty. When one is condemned spiritually, that person is separated from God for eternity. Since God condemned sin through the death of Jesus, those who are joined to Christ are removed from condemnation forever. Only the Judge can condemn, and he has done everything that is required to deliver us from condemnation. When we receive Christ, we receive God's pardon from condemnation. Now there is NO condemnation!

"law of the Spirit of life"—This expression denotes the liberating power of the Holy Spirit exerted through the life, death, and resurrection of Jesus Christ. The Spirit sets us free from the power of sin and the spiritual death that results from sin.

"sinful nature"—Sometimes translated "flesh," this word can refer to the physical body (1 Cor. 6:16) or to human beings in general (Rom. 3:20). The word is used here, however, to describe the condition or situation of people outside of Jesus Christ (i.e., spiritual bondage). As Christians we are no longer in this condition, and we should not live as if we are.

Why We Fight

In one of the last episodes of the World War II series *Band of Brothers*, Easy Company scouts the area surrounding a German town they have recently occupied. The American soldiers are totally unprepared for what they discover. Outside of town they stumble onto a prison camp for Polish Jews. The camp is filled with disease and death. Battle-hardened soldiers stare in disbelief as they behold the work of Satan and sin. No wonder they labeled this particular episode, "Why We Fight." In the same way, Jesus came to destroy the Devil's work (1 John 3:8) and set people free.

Source of Freedom

John 8:31–59 records an intense conversation between Jesus and the Jewish religious leaders. Notice how much he talks about slavery and freedom in verses 31–36:

To the Jews who had believed him, Jesus said, "If you hold to my teaching, you are really my disciples. Then you will know the truth, and the truth will set you free." They answered him, "We are Abraham's descendants and have never been slaves of anyone. How can you say that we shall be set free?" Jesus replied, "I tell you the truth, everyone who sins is a slave to sin. Now a slave has no permanent place in the family, but a son belongs to it forever. So if the Son sets you free, you will be free indeed."

—John 8:31–36

Cross-References

Jer. 31:31–34; Ezek. 11:17–20; 36:24–27; Luke 4:18–19; John 3:18; 8:31–36; Rom. 5–8; 2 Cor. 3:17–18; Gal. 3–5; Eph. 2:1–5; Col. 1:13–14; Titus 3:3; Heb. 2:14–15; 10:17–23; 1 Peter 2:16; 2 Peter 2:19

For Deeper Study

Cloud, Henry, and John Townsend. *How People Grow.* Grand Rapids: Zondervan, 2001.

Fee, Gordon D. *God's Empowering Presence.* Peabody, MA: Hendrickson, 1994.

Moo, Douglas J. *Romans.* NIV Application Commentary. Grand Rapids: Zondervan, 2000.

So What?

1. If you are "in Christ," you are free from condemnation. God is for you, not against you! Do you ever catch yourself thinking that God still wants to condemn you now or plans to condemn you at the final judgment? If you are still expecting condemnation, what else could God do to convince you that you are free?

2. What is God's goal in setting us free from the law of sin and death?

3. Even Christians can sometimes become enslaved again when they choose to live according to the flesh instead of according to the Spirit. What things or people tend to enslave you these days?

4. What is one practical step you could take this week to live in freedom rather than bondage? How can your Christian community help you?

5. What has the Lord been saying to you through this last series: Belief About Satan and Sin → Behavior in Spiritual Warfare → Becoming Free?

The Word Became Flesh

Jesus Christ

The heart of the Christian faith is a person. In a real sense Christianity *is* Jesus Christ. Our faith in Jesus includes accepting his teachings, trusting his death on the cross for us, believing that God raised him from the dead, and looking forward to his future return. But our faith in Jesus all starts with recognizing who he is. The rescue story begins with God meeting us where we are. When God the Son became a human being, God came looking for us. The technical term for God becoming a man is *incarnation,* a word that means "being in flesh." Think for a second about why God had to become a human.

Sin caused a break in our relationship with God. Like Adam and Eve, we hid from God in our shame and fear. Yet because of God's great compassion, he came after us—not to condemn us, but to heal us and offer us a way home. God sent his Son to rescue us from Satan and sin and restore us to a right relationship with him.

> For God so loved the world that he gave his one and only Son, that whoever believes in him shall not perish but have eternal life. For God did not send his Son into the world to condemn the world, but to save the world through him. (John 3:16–17)

In order to rescue us, God the Son became a flesh-and-blood human being—Jesus of Nazareth. The Son has always existed and is completely equal to God the Father. He is the eternal Son of God (one person) who is at the same time fully God and fully man (two natures). John 1:14 puts it this way, "The Word became flesh." Philip Yancey learned more about God becoming a human being (incarnation) from, of all things, his pet fish.

> I learned about incarnation when I kept a salt-water aquarium. Management of a marine aquarium, I discovered, is no easy task. I had to run a portable chemical laboratory to monitor the nitrate levels and the ammonia content. I pumped in vitamins and antibodies and

sulfa drugs and enough enzymes to make a rock grow. I filtered the water through glass fibers and charcoal, and exposed it to ultraviolet light. You would think, in view of all the energy expended on their behalf, that my fish would at least be grateful. Not so. Every time my shadow loomed above the tank they dove for cover into the nearest shell. They showed me one "emotion" only: fear. Although I opened the lid and dropped in food on a regular schedule, three times a day, they responded to each visit as a sure sign of my designs to torture them. I could not convince them of my true concern.

To my fish I was deity. I was too large for them, my actions too incomprehensible. My acts of mercy they saw as cruelty; my attempts at healing they viewed as destruction. To change their perceptions, I began to see, would require a form of incarnation. I would have to become a fish and "speak" to them in a language they could understand.

A human being becoming a fish is nothing compared to God becoming a baby. And yet according to the Gospels that is what happened at Bethlehem. The God who created matter took shape within it, as an artist might become a spot on a painting or a playwright a character within his own play. God wrote a story, only using real characters, on the pages of real history. The Word became flesh. (*The Jesus I Never Knew*, 38–39)

The early Christians concluded that Jesus was completely divine and completely human. In the process they rejected these two defective explanations of the Incarnation:

- Adoptionism—The belief that God the Father adopted a man (Jesus) to be his Son. This took place at his baptism, and sometime later (probably at the cross), God abandoned the man Jesus.
- Docetism—The view that Jesus was a divine being who only pretended to be a real man. Jesus wasn't really human; he just appeared to be human. He was God putting on a human suit.

Both of these views were rejected because they fail to explain what the Gospels tell us, and because they leave us without a real savior. If Jesus was not both human and divine, he could not rescue us from Satan and sin. *If he was just a man*, he could not save us since he also would need someone to save him. *If he was not a man*, he would have no real connection to us as humans and wouldn't be able to die a real death for our sins.

To be able to reconnect us to God, Jesus had to be both divine and human. Since he is human, he can sympathize with us, experience what it means to be human, suffer, and die. Since he is divine, he can live a sinless life and his death on the cross can pay the just penalty for sin. God himself then provides the sacrifice that he requires.

JESUS IS GOD	JESUS IS HUMAN
Claimed to be God (John 19:7)	Said he was a man (John 8:40)
Addressed as Lord (Acts 2:36)	Human ancestors (Matt. 1)
Eternal (John 8:58)	Had a real body (1 John 1:1)
One with Father (John 10:30)	Grew and developed (Luke 2)
Authority to forgive (Luke 5)	Became hungry, thirsty, and tired (John 4)
Performed miracles (Mark 4–5)	Was tempted (Matt. 4:1)
Recognized as Lord (Rom. 10:9)	Sinless human (Heb. 4:15)
Disciples saw as God (Matt. 20)	Sorrowful and troubled (Matt. 26:37)
Sinless (2 Cor. 5:21; 1 John 3:5)	Suffered and died (John 19)
Worshiped as God (Matt. 28)	
Crucified for claims (Mark 14–15)	
Raised from the dead (Luke 24)	

In Believing 7 we will discover more about Jesus' death and resurrection. For now, let's take a closer look at the Word becoming flesh as described in John 1.

A Closer Look—John 1:1–3, 14, 18

Begin by reading John 1:1–18 in your Bible. Then carefully study the passage below. Circle repeated words, identify lists, underline prepositional phrases, note characteristics of the Word, and so on. Jot down your observations in the margins.

"made his dwelling"—During the wilderness wanderings of Israel, God made his presence known in a temporary tent called a tabernacle. God filled that tent with his presence and his glory. John 1:14 literally says the Word (Jesus) "tabernacled" or "pitched his tent" among us. God came to live among us in the person of Jesus Christ. The same word is used again in Revelation 21:3, where we are told that God will make his permanent home among his people in the new heaven and new earth.

"made him known"—No one has seen God the Father, but God the Son has revealed, or explained, him. This word literally means "to exegete," or lead out. Jesus Christ leads out, or makes known, the heart of the invisible God. Only Jesus Christ, who has the very nature of God, can really show us what the Father is like. If you want to know what God is like, look at Jesus.

SCRIPTURE NOTES

¹In the beginning was the Word, and the Word was with God, and the Word was God. ²He was with God in the beginning. ³Through him all things were made; without him nothing was made that has been made. . . . ¹⁴The Word became flesh and made his dwelling among us. We have seen his glory, the glory of the One and Only, who came from the Father, full of grace and truth. . . . ¹⁸No one has ever seen God, but God the One and Only, who is at the Father's side, has made him known.

The Greek word for **fish** is ΙΧΘΥΣ (*Ichthus*). It was used by early Christians as an acronym that spoke of Jesus and his mission.

Ι — Jesus
Χ — Christ
Θ — God's
Υ — Son
Σ — Savior

What's in a Name?

"**Jesus**"—The angel told Joseph, "You are to give him the name Jesus, because he will save his people from their sins" (Matt. 1:21). The name "Jesus" literally means "The Lord saves." Jesus came to rescue or save us from Satan and sin.

"**Christ**"—This is not Jesus' last name but a title, "the Christ." The term "Christ" (Greek) is equivalent to "Messiah" (Hebrew), or "anointed one." In the Old Testament the person anointed with oil was singled out by God as being very important and having a special mission. Over time, the term *Christ* came to mean something more like "deliverer" or "rescuer." Again, Jesus is the one who will deliver his people from their enemies.

Crossing the Bridge

From your careful study of the verses on page 95, what messages does God seem to be communicating through this text? Write out present-tense statements that (a) reflect what the text says and means and (b) apply equally to the ancient audience and the contemporary audience. Sometimes biblical principles relate to who God is rather than what we are supposed to do.

- Jesus Christ is fully God and existed as God before time began ("in the beginning," cf. Gen. 1:1).

- Jesus Christ was involved in creation ("through him all things were made").

-

-

-

So What?

1. Jesus himself is a picture of God. As you think about what Jesus said and did, what is the most meaningful aspect of that portrait for you? In other words, in what ways does reading about Jesus help you understand God?

2. Why did Jesus have to be 100 percent God and 100 percent man in order to rescue us from Satan and sin?

3. Which is more difficult for you to believe—that Jesus is fully divine or fully human? Why?

4. What would you say is the most comforting element of Jesus being a real human being—that he was tempted, that he suffered, or what?

5. What are some ways that we can live "incarnational" lives as believers?

Cross-References
Matt. 1:23; Luke 1:35; John 10:30–38; Rom. 8:3; 9:5; Gal. 4:4–5; Phil. 2:5–11; Col. 1:15, 19; 2:2–9; Titus 2:13; Heb. 1:1–3; 2:14; 1 John 1:1–4; 4:2; 5:20; Rev. 1:5–6; 5:12–13

For Deeper Study
Bock, Darrell L. *Jesus According to Scripture.* Grand Rapids: Baker, 2002.
Erickson, Millard J. *The Word Became Flesh: A Contemporary Incarnational Christology.* Grand Rapids: Baker, 1991.
McGrath, Alister E. *I Believe.* Downers Grove, IL: InterVarsity Press, 1997.
Morris, Leon. *The Gospel According to John.* Rev. ed. New International Commentary on the New Testament. Grand Rapids: Eerdmans, 1995.

The Cost of Discipleship

Following

Dietrich Bonhoeffer, a German pastor during the second World War, was eventually hanged by the Nazis for his resistance against that evil regime. In his book, *The Cost of Discipleship,* Bonhoeffer wrote, "The cross is laid on every Christian. . . . When Christ calls a man, He bids him come and die" (page 99). In Believing 6 we focused on our belief that God the Son became a human being in order to rescue us, that he lived a sinless life, died on the cross as our substitute, and was raised from the dead. Now we will see that the same Jesus who gave his all for us demands that we give our all to him. His gift to us is also his demand of us. Grace is free, but it is not cheap. In this study we turn our attention to the habit of choosing to follow Jesus in every area of life.

Take a moment and read Mark 8:27–9:1, the context for our focal passage. You will notice that Simon Peter answers Jesus' question correctly (8:29—"You are the Christ") only to be rebuked a few minutes later (8:33—"Get behind me, Satan!"). Imagine for a moment that you are Simon Peter and that you are making your journal entry at the end of this very confusing day. What would you write?

As Jesus moves closer to dying on the cross, he begins to teach his followers about the kind of Rescuer (Messiah, or Christ) he came to be. The disciples, like other Jewish people of Jesus' day, expected the Messiah to liberate them from Roman rule. They expected a political or military Messiah. No doubt, Jesus shocks them with the news that he will suffer and die in Jerusalem. The problem is that they cannot conceive of a "crucified messiah." According to their way of thinking, deliverers don't get themselves crucified and conquering kings don't go down in defeat.

Surprisingly, when Jesus tells them about his own impending rejection and death, he adds a few sentences about a cross they would have to carry. To be sure, only Jesus could carry his cross to Calvary to die for the sins of humanity, but he's not the only one who must carry a cross.

A Closer Look—Mark 8:34–38

Carefully study the following passage by answering the standard story questions—Who? What? When? Where? Why? and How? Write your answers and observations below.

"deny himself"—This does not refer to denying something to ourselves but to denying ourselves the right to control life. Self-denial means saying "no" to selfish desires and ambitions so that we may say "yes" to Jesus.

"take up his cross"—This is not talking about the burdens that all humans bear (e.g., an illness or a difficult relative) but about our willingness to face rejection and ridicule because we follow Jesus.

SCRIPTURE NOTES

³⁴Then he called the crowd to him along with his disciples and said: "If anyone would come after me, he must deny himself and take up his cross and follow me. ³⁵For whoever wants to save his life will lose it, but whoever loses his life for me and for the gospel will save it. ³⁶What good is it for a man to gain the whole world, yet forfeit his soul? ³⁷Or what can a man give in exchange for his soul? ³⁸If anyone is ashamed of me and my words in this adulterous and sinful generation, the Son of Man will be ashamed of him when he comes in his Father's glory with the holy angels."

Crossing the Bridge

From your careful study of Mark 8:34–38, you can begin to see what God is trying to say through this text. In the space provided, write out several principles that capture the timeless truths God is communicating through these verses.

- People must choose to follow Jesus Christ. He will not force them to follow.

- The requirements are the same for everyone who chooses to follow Christ—deny self, take up the cross, and follow.

BEHAVING 6—*Following*

•

•

•

A *disciple* is a committed follower of a teacher or leader. The Pharisees had disciples (Matt. 22:15–16; Mark 2:18), as did John the Baptist (Mark 2:18; John 1:35; 3:25). If you study the New Testament thoroughly, you will discover what Michael Wilkins calls the nonnegotiables of biblical discipleship (*In His Image*, 61).

- It is grounded in a personal, costly relationship with Jesus.
- It results in a new identity in Jesus.
- It is guided by God's Word.
- It is empowered by the Holy Spirit.
- It is developed through a whole-life process.
- It is practiced in communities of faith.
- It is carried out in our everyday world.

Under "Cross-References" you will find a list of verses that relate to the topic of discipleship. Look up each of those texts and jot down your insights about the costs and blessings of following Jesus.

COSTS	BLESSINGS

So What?

1. Select one of the principles that you wrote earlier. How do you need to think differently or live differently in order to experience that truth more consistently in your life?

2. What is the most difficult aspect of "self" for you to deny?

3. List some specific costs of following Jesus in these areas of your life:

- family

- work or school

- relationships

- leisure time

- money

- eating habits

- attitudes

-

-

4. How do we know when rejection by others is caused by bearing the cross of genuine discipleship or when the ridicule stems from our own obnoxious and foolish ways?

5. In light of the context, what does Mark 8:36 mean for Peter and the other disciples? Have you ever had an expectation about how the Christian life should work that was either not fulfilled or was fulfilled in a different way?

Carrying a Rugged Cross

Jesus has many lovers of his heavenly kingdom these days, but few of them carry his cross. He has many who desire comfort, few who desire affliction. He has many friends to share his meals, but few to share his fasts. Everyone is eager to rejoice with him, but few are willing to endure anything for him. Many follow Jesus up to the breaking of bread, but few as far as drinking from the chalice of his passion. Many love Jesus as long as no difficulties touch them. Many praise and bless him as long as they receive comfort from him.

—Thomas à Kempis,
Imitation of Christ, 2.11

Cross-References

Matt. 7:24–27; 10:37–39; 11:29–30; 16:13–28; Mark 3:31–35; 10:29–31; Luke 6:22–23; 9:22–27, 59–62; 14:25–33; John 8:31–32; 14:21; 15:11, 21–22; 16:33; 20:19

For Deeper Study

Bonhoeffer, Dietrich. *The Cost of Discipleship.* New York: Macmillan, 1963.

Garland, David E. *Mark.* NIV Application Commentary. Grand Rapids: Zondervan, 1996.

Ogden, Greg. *Transforming Discipleship: Making Disciples a Few at a Time.* Downers Grove, IL: InterVarsity Press, 2003.

Out with the Old, In with the New

New Identity in Christ

God came to us in Jesus Christ. "The Word became flesh." He entered our world so that we might enter his world and experience the perfect love and fellowship that comes only from the triune God. Wow! Jesus is God incarnate, fully God and fully man. He came to us in order to rescue us from Satan and sin and give us real life. He came to give his all—yet the one who gave his all for us also demands our all. He calls us to deny ourselves, take up our cross, and follow him. Following Christ is costly and affects the very core of who we are. Christ followers take on a whole new identity. We become brand-new people. As the apostle Paul says, "If anyone is in Christ, he is a new creation; the old has gone, the new has come!" (2 Cor. 5:17). Our new identity in Christ is the subject of Becoming 6.

Have you ever failed God? It's not a pleasant thought, but sometimes we learn as much (or more) from our failures as we do from our successes. That is the case with a man we read about in the New Testament, a man who boasted far beyond his ability to be faithful. (Not that we've ever done that!) You'll recall that it was Simon Peter who rebuked Jesus when the Lord told his disciples that he had to go to Jerusalem to suffer and die (Mark 8:31–32). Peter couldn't conceive of a savior or rescuer who would get himself killed. Jesus' response was blunt and uncompromising, "Get behind me, Satan!" he said. "You do not have in mind the things of God, but the things of men" (Mark 8:33). Jesus would win the victory over sin and Satan, but he would do it God's way—not by military might or by political scheming, but by sacrificing his own life on a cruel cross. He would take our punishment, so that we (the guilty sinners) might receive his pardon. God's way is victory through sacrifice.

Even after a harsh rebuke, Peter kept on walking the road of self-sufficiency. He continued to hold on to his own dreams and expectations about how God should behave more than what Jesus was revealing to him. The night before he died on the cross, Jesus ate a last supper with his disciples. That evening Peter again boasted about his ability to remain faithful even though all others might fail.

> Then Jesus told them, "This very night you will all fall away on account of me. . . . But after I have risen, I will go ahead of you into Galilee." Peter replied, *"Even if all fall away on account of you, I never will."* "I tell you the truth," Jesus answered, "this very night, before the rooster crows, you will disown me three times." But Peter declared, *"Even if I have to die with you, I will never disown you."* And all the other disciples said the same. (Matt. 26:31–35)

The next phase of the story is rather famous. Within hours after his boast, Peter denies Jesus three times. Jesus was right, of course, and he does go to Jerusalem to suffer and die on a cross. On the third day, Jesus is raised from the dead—God wins his way!

A Closer Look—John 21:15–23

What about Simon Peter? He had rebuked Jesus and received a rebuke in return. He had boasted naively that he would stay faithful, but he had failed miserably. Jesus had done things his way, and now Peter was lost and confused. Yet Jesus was not finished with Simon Peter. (Take a minute to read John 21:1–14.) After breakfast, Jesus and Peter have a brief but historic conversation (John 21:15–17) that consists of three questions, three answers, and three challenges or affirmations.

3 QUESTIONS from Jesus	3 ANSWERS from Peter	3 CHALLENGES from Jesus
"Simon son of John, do you truly love *[agapē]* me more than these?"	"Yes, Lord," he said, "you know that I love *[phileō]* you."	"Feed my lambs."
"Simon son of John, do you truly love *[agapē]* me?"	"Yes, Lord, you know that I love *[phileō]* you."	"Take care of my sheep."
"Simon son of John, do you love *[phileō]* me?"	"Lord, you know all things; you know that I love *[phileō]* you."	"Feed my sheep."

John Ortberg captures the significance of the event as Peter comes to grips with his new identity in Christ:

> Now it's just Jesus and Peter before a little fire, a charcoal fire. "Simon, son of John . . ." Jesus doesn't even use his old nickname, Peter. He uses his formal name, as if to say, "I won't presume that

"fire of burning coals"—Interestingly, there are only two places in the New Testament where this expression is used. First, in John 18:18 we are told that Peter is standing by a "charcoal fire" (NASB) warming himself when he denies Christ the first time. Second, we read in John 21:9 that Jesus cooks breakfast for the disciples over a "charcoal fire" (NASB). Isn't it just like Jesus to consider the sights and smells of denial when creating the setting for restoration?

"do you love me?"—Two verbs for love are used in the questions and answers in this passage—*agapē* and *phileō* (see the chart to the left). Some writers suggest that *agapē* refers to God's kind of love while *phileō* refers to human love. Since both verbs are used in the New Testament of the Father's love for the Son, this distinction does not really hold up. Word meanings always depend on the specific context rather than on a dictionary definition. Here in John 21, Jesus seems to use these verbs interchangeably to simply mean "love." He also uses different words for "know," "feed/take care," and "lambs/sheep." We shouldn't think that Peter finally brings Jesus down to his level when Jesus switches from *agapē* to *phileō* in the final question. The two words are used simply to keep things interesting. God enjoys variety.

you want the old intimate relationship. I won't presume you still want to wear the name I gave you."

"Simon, son of John, do you love me?" Now Jesus is the vulnerable one. Now Jesus is the Lover waiting to hear the response of the one he loves. "Yes, Lord," Peter answers, but he doesn't fully trust his ability to assess even his own heart. You know everything. You know. I understand Peter's answer: Lord you know. As best I can, I do love you. When I'm in my right mind, I do. I want to, better than I do now. I don't even know the whole truth about my heart. Lord, you know.

"Then feed my sheep," Jesus says. Love and teach and guard and guide and serve the little flock that means all the world to me. Get back in the game. Three times this is repeated, until Peter is hurt. Why does Jesus keep asking? . . .

The significance of the repetition is not in the synonyms but in the number of times the question is repeated. Three times. Peter does not know what we do, that he is being healed by the Lord of a second chance. Not once but three times he stood by the [charcoal] fire and denied his Lord; not once but three times he stands by the fire and professes his love. Jesus says to Peter, Jesus says to everyone who's ever stood by the fire and failed God, Jesus says still to you and me whatever we've done, "Get back in the game. Nurture the gifts I gave you and cherish the calling I gave you and devote yourself to the church. Feed my sheep. They need you." (*Love Beyond Reason*, 68–69)

Just as Peter worked through failure to a new understanding of his relationship with Jesus, so we too have the opportunity to hear God speak to us about who we are. Begin by writing down seven good things about yourself and seven bad things. These can be physical, emotional, mental, or whatever. This practical idea comes from Michael Wilkins (see *In His Image*, 81–88).

Good Things About Yourself	Bad Things About Yourself
1.	1.
2.	2.
3.	3.
4.	4.
5.	5.
6.	6.
7.	7.

Wilkins says that knowing ourselves is a good place to start developing our identity in Christ. He encourages us to avoid the trap of comparing ourselves with others and go ahead and accept ourselves—"OK, like everyone else, I have some good and some bad. I'm not going to focus on either one. Instead, I trust God to use my strengths and transform my weaknesses by the power of his Spirit." Wilkins suggests that we *build on the good* and *grow away from the bad*" by absorbing the truth of Scripture, forgetting about ourselves, connecting with God's community, and going public with our new identity.

Why not check out what God says about who you are "in Christ." (Some of you hate to look up verses, but you do other things that you hate, like shaving, so give this a try.) What do these Scriptures say about our new identity in Christ?

- John 1:12–13

- Romans 6:23; 1 Corinthians 15:22; 1 Thessalonians 4:16

- Romans 8:1

- Romans 8:38–39

- Romans 12:5; Galatians 3:28

- 1 Corinthians 1:2

- 1 Corinthians 1:4; Ephesians 2:7; 2 Timothy 1:9; 2:1

- 2 Corinthians 3:14

- 2 Corinthians 5:19; Ephesians 2:13

- Galatians 2:4

- Galatians 2:16

- Galatians 2:20; Colossians 3:3–4

- Galatians 3:26

- Ephesians 1:3

Stop Comparing!
Even after Peter had been restored by Jesus, Peter had the nerve to start comparing himself with John, another follower. Jesus tells Peter to stop it—"Jesus answered, 'If I want him [John] to remain alive until I return, what is that to you? You [Peter] must follow me'" (John 21:22). Are you always comparing yourself with other people? The same people? Why do you do it? God hates comparison because somebody always loses when we compare. How can you stop comparing?

- Ephesians 1:11

- Ephesians 1:13

- Ephesians 2:10

- Ephesians 4:32

- Philippians 3:9

- Philippians 4:7; 1 Peter 5:14

- Colossians 2:9–10

- 2 Timothy 2:1

- 1 Peter 1:23; 2:9

So What?

1. Jesus used Simon Peter's failure to help Peter understand who he really was. Have you ever given your failures to God? What other life circumstances has God used most effectively to shape your identity?

2. Of all the Scriptures that describe our new identity in Christ, which ones are the most meaningful to you at this point in your life? Why?

3. As you think about the good and bad things you wrote about yourself, can you think of a few specific ways to "build on the good and grow from the bad"?

4. Read the quote from Boyd in the sidebar on page 106. In essence the apostle Paul is saying, "Be who you are." Why is it important that God always sees our behavior arising from our identity and not the other way around?

5. What has helped you more than anything else to see yourself as the new person you are in Christ?

6. How can the members of your community group help each other embrace their new identity in Christ and live accordingly?

Cross-References
See the list of "in Christ" verses on pages 105–6.

For Deeper Study
Ortberg, John. *Love Beyond Reason: Moving God's Love from Your Head to Your Heart.* Grand Rapids: Zondervan, 1998.
Stott, John. *Life in Christ.* Wheaton, IL: Tyndale House, 1991.
Wilkins, Michael J. *In His Image: Reflecting Christ in Everyday Life.* Colorado Springs: NavPress, 1997.

I Boast No More

Salvation

The Danish philosopher Søren Kierkegaard tells a story about how God's love moved him to come to our rescue.

Imagine there was a king that loved a humble maiden. She had no royal pedigree, no education, no standing in the court. She dressed in rags. She lived in a shack. She led the ragged life of a peasant. But for reasons no one could ever quite figure out, the king fell in love with this girl, in the way kings sometimes do. Why he should love her is beyond explaining, but love her he did. And he could not stop loving her.

Then there awoke in the heart of the king an anxious thought. How was he to reveal his love to the girl? How could he bridge the chasm of station and position that separated them? His advisers, of course, would tell him to simply command her to be his queen. For he was a man of immense power—every statesman feared his wrath, every foreign power trembled before him, every courtier groveled in the dust at the king's voice. She would have no power to resist; she would owe him an eternal debt of gratitude.

But power—even unlimited power—cannot command love. He could force her body to be present in his palace; he could not force her love for him to be present in her heart. He might be able to gain her obedience this way, but coerced submission is not what he wanted. He longed for intimacy of heart and oneness of spirit. All the power in the world cannot unlock the door to the human heart. It must be opened from the inside. His advisers might suggest that the king give up this love, give his heart to a more worthy woman. But this the king will not do, cannot do. And so his love is also his pain. . . .

The king could try to bridge the chasm between them by elevating her to his position. He could shower her with gifts, dress her in purple and silk, have her crowned queen. But if he brought her to his palace, if he radiated the sun of his magnificence over her, if she saw all the wealth and power and pomp of his greatness, she would be overwhelmed. How would he know (or she either, for that matter) if she loved him for himself or for all that he gave her? How could she know that he loved her and would love her still even if she had remained only a humble peasant? . . .

Every other alternative came to nothing. There was only one way. So one day the king rose, left his throne, removed his crown, relinquished his scepter, and laid aside his royal robes. He took upon himself the life of a peasant. He dressed in rags, scratched out a living in the dirt, groveled for food, dwelt in a shack. He did not just take on the outward appearance of a servant, it became his actual life, his nature, his burden. He became as ragged as the one he loved, so that she could be united to him forever. It was the only way. (quoted in Ortberg, *Love Beyond Reason*, 201–2)

The grand story of Scripture begins with God—Father, Son, and Spirit—living in perfect fellowship. Because of his great love for us and his desire that we experience his perfect community, God sent his Son to rescue us from Satan and sin and to bring us into a right relationship with him. In Believing 7 we will focus on *salvation*—what God has done in Jesus Christ to draw us to himself.

The salvation that God accomplished through Christ can be summarized in two movements, *humiliation* and *exaltation*, both of which are described powerfully in Philippians 2:5–11.

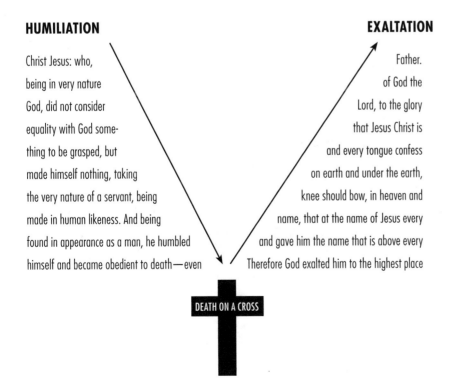

HUMILIATION

Christ Jesus: who, being in very nature God, did not consider equality with God something to be grasped, but made himself nothing, taking the very nature of a servant, being made in human likeness. And being found in appearance as a man, he humbled himself and became obedient to death—even

DEATH ON A CROSS

EXALTATION

Father.
of God the
Lord, to the glory
that Jesus Christ is
and every tongue confess
on earth and under the earth,
knee should bow, in heaven and
name, that at the name of Jesus every
and gave him the name that is above every
Therefore God exalted him to the highest place

There are many important words related to the topic of salvation. Here are just a few.

Salvation—The totality of what God has done in Christ to rescue us from sin and Satan. Salvation has three "tenses"—we **have been** saved from the penalty of sin, we **are being** saved from the power of sin, and we **will be** saved from the presence of sin.

Justification—A legal term meaning to acquit or declare a person to be just (i.e., not guilty). When we are justified, we are restored to a state of righteousness based on our trust in the grace shown us in Jesus Christ. The opposite of justification is condemnation (Rom. 8:1).

Reconciliation—This term speaks of restoring a personal relationship or renewing a friendship. When we accept Christ, we are no longer God's enemies. Rather, God adopts us as his children (John 1:12).

Redemption—This business term refers to the payment of a ransom in order to purchase a person's freedom (slavery being the original context). Jesus paid the price to ransom us from sin (Mark 10:45).

Sanctification—The process by which people who have been justified are changed and transformed into the likeness of Christ by the power of the Spirit (Rom. 12:1–2).

Glorification—The final step in salvation, when we are made like Christ and live with him forever (Phil. 3:20–21).

The Lamb of God

He was despised and rejected by men, a man of sorrows, and familiar with suffering. Like one from whom men hide their faces he was despised, and we esteemed him not. Surely he took up our infirmities and carried our sorrows, yet we considered him stricken by God, smitten by him, and afflicted. But he was pierced for our transgressions, he was crushed for our iniquities; the punishment that brought us peace was upon him, and by his wounds we are healed. We all, like sheep, have gone astray, each of us has turned to his own way; and the LORD has laid on him the iniquity of us all. He was oppressed and afflicted, yet he did not open his mouth; he was led like a lamb to the slaughter, and as a sheep before her shearers is silent, so he did not open his mouth.

—Isaiah 53:3–7

Jesus' *humiliation* involves a downward progression—he becomes a man, then a man who is a servant, then a servant-man who dies, then a servant-man who dies the most humiliating death known to humans—crucifixion. But why did Jesus have to die?

The answer relates to who we are and who God is. We are sinful, guilty people, totally unable to do anything to rescue ourselves (read Eph. 2:1–3). In contrast, God is the holy Creator and Judge who must condemn sin. And yet God loves us and desires a relationship with us. How could God act in a way that would satisfy his holy love? How could he condemn our sin *and* still have a relationship with us? God's answer was the cross! On the cross, God took the penalty for sin (death) on himself, so that we might experience his forgiveness. Jesus Christ died in our place, as our substitute. Jesus applied Isaiah 53 to himself and understood his death as a sin-bearing death (see "The Lamb of God" in the sidebar). Paul writes, "While we were still sinners, Christ died for us" (Rom. 5:8). The beauty of the cross is that Jesus took our curse (Gal. 3:13) and bore our sin (2 Cor. 5:21) so that he might set us free from sin and restore our relationship to him. As Charles Wesley wrote in his famous hymn "And Can It Be That I Should Gain?" "Amazing love! How can it be that Thou, my God, should'st died for me?"

The second movement in salvation is *exaltation*, which includes both the resurrection and the ascension. The resurrection is the cornerstone of the Christian faith. Paul is right, "If Christ has not been raised, your faith is futile; you are still in your sins" (1 Cor. 15:17). If you want to read more about the reality of the resurrection, see Lee Strobel's *The Case for the Resurrection.* If you want to dig even deeper, the definitive work is N. T. Wright's, *The Resurrection of the Son of God.* Forty days after his resurrection, Jesus ascended to the Father, where he is now seated at his right hand, crowned with glory and honor (Col. 3:1; Heb. 2:7–9) and interceding for us (Rom. 8:34; Heb. 7:25). To help us focus on the essentials of salvation, we turn to Ephesians 2:8–10.

A Closer Look—Ephesians 2:8–10

Take a minute and read Ephesians 2:1–10 to get a feel for the context. Notice how this text moves from death to life, from slavery to freedom, from self-gratification to service. It's like taking a trip from Death Valley to Mount Everest. Actually, that journey doesn't begin to compare with the reality you read about in this short paragraph. As you reflect on God's Word on page 111, look carefully at each callout box, where the meaning is explained.

God's grace is the *basis* or source of salvation.

[8]For it is by grace you have been saved,

Emphasizes the ongoing results of our salvation and could be translated, "you are saved."

Faith is not a human "work" that earns God's gift of salvation, but faith is the *means* by which we receive salvation.

through faith—and this not from yourselves,

The word "this" refers to the whole idea of salvation by grace through faith (the first part of v. 8) and not just to the word "faith." The whole thing is a "gift from God."

it is the gift of God—[9]not by works,

Here the word "boast" refers to an attitude of presumption and confidence before God based on our own achievements. Since salvation is a gift, who can boast?

so that no one can boast. [10]For we are

"Works" refers to human effort or activities aimed at earning salvation. Salvation is "by grace," not "by works."

God's workmanship, created in Christ Jesus

"Workmanship" refers to the work of a craftsman or artist. It is often used in the Old Testament to refer to God's work of creating the world. Believers are God's new creation, his new masterpiece.

The *goal* of being created in Christ is good works. We don't achieve salvation by good works (the basis is grace), but our salvation should result in good works.

to do good works, which God prepared

in advance for us to do.

We have not been saved to wait passively for heaven. God designed us to literally "walk in" good works. We walk in what God has prepared ahead of time for our present life.

Crossing the Bridge

What biblical principles do you see in Ephesians 2:8–10?

- There is absolutely nothing we can do to earn or merit salvation.

- Even though God offers salvation as a gift (by grace), we still need to receive the gift through faith for it to make any difference in our lives.

-

-

So What?

1. Which "power word" in this study's sidebar (page 109) means the most to you at this point in your life? Why?

The Great Exchange

How then could God express simultaneously his holiness in judgment and his love in pardon? Only by providing a divine substitute for the sinner, so that the substitute would receive the judgment and the sinner the pardon. . . . [God] was unwilling to act in love at the expense of his holiness or in holiness at the expense of his love. So we may say that he satisfied his holy love by himself dying the death and so bearing the judgment which sinners deserved.

—John Stott, *Cross of Christ,* 134, 152

Cross-References

Mark 10:45; John 3:1–16; Rom. 3–5; 6:23; 10:8–10; 1 Cor. 15; 2 Cor. 5:11–21; Gal. 2:20; Col. 1:19–23; 1 Tim. 2:5–6; 2 Tim. 1:9–10; Heb. 7:27; 9:11–28; 1 Peter 1:18–21; 2:22–24; 3:18

For Deeper Study

Akers, John, John Woodbridge, and Kevin G. Harney. *This We Believe: The Good News of Jesus Christ for the World.* Grand Rapids: Zondervan, 2000.

Hoehner, Harold W. *Ephesians.* Grand Rapids: Baker, 2002.

Stott, John R. W. *The Cross of Christ.* Downers Grove, IL: InterVarsity Press, 1986.

Strobel, Lee. *The Case for the Resurrection.* Grand Rapids: Zondervan, 1998.

Wright, N. T. *The Resurrection of the Son of God.* Minneapolis: Fortress, 2003.

2. How has God removed our right to boast about our salvation?

3. What hits you the hardest about Christ's descent from the throne to the cross?

4. The means of experiencing salvation is faith. What is included in saving faith?

5. Do you know of any helpful illustrations that clarify the role of faith in our experience of salvation?

6. Does the fact that salvation has three tenses help you in your walk with Christ (see "Salvation" in the sidebar on page 109)? Why or why not?

7. Explain one of your biblical principles (see "Crossing the Bridge" on page 111) to a group of your Christian friends.

Working Out What God Works In

Trusting and Acting

Salvation is everything that God has done in Christ to rescue us from sin and Satan. Our focal text in the last study, Ephesians 2:8–10, shows us that salvation is *by grace* (the basis) *through faith* (the means) *for good works* (the result). As we think about how salvation is made real in our lives, the next question is this—What is the relationship between faith and works? In other words, whose job is spiritual growth? What am I supposed to do, and what should I trust God to do? Some people believe that God does it all as we simply wait on him to transform our lives. At the other extreme, you'll find people who focus almost exclusively on willpower and activity. The biblical truth lies between these two extremes of complete passivity and stubborn self-reliance. In Behaving 7 we will explore the habit of trusting and acting and how they work together to connect us to God.

The relationship between faith and works can be confusing. Consider the apparent contradiction between what Paul says and what James says:

Galatians 2:16		James 2:24
So we, too, have put our faith in Christ Jesus that we may be justified by faith in Christ and not by observing the law, because by observing the law no one will be justified.	*vs.*	You see that a person is justified by what he does and not by faith alone.

"work out"—This word means to "do" or "produce" or "accomplish" something. In the New Testament we are assured that suffering "produces" perseverance (Rom. 5:3), and we read about what Christ has "accomplished" through the apostle Paul (Rom. 15:18). The word translated "work out" here in Philippians 2 is a command. Although we can do nothing to save ourselves, we are not merely passive spectators. The Christian faith is not an "auto-pilot" kind of faith. Instead, we are to be active and involved in allowing God to do his mighty work in us.

Well, are people justified by faith or by what they do? If you read Galatians and James carefully, you will notice that the context helps to answer this question. In Galatians, Paul is facing a situation where people are thinking about replacing the gospel of grace with a false gospel based on religious works. Paul's point is that we can be justified only by relying on the work of Christ and not by trusting in our own ability. James, on the other hand, is talking to people who think that faith and works can be separated (2:18). James stresses that real faith results in good works or it is not real faith. In reality, Paul and James are like two soldiers standing back to back fighting the same enemy. You may notice as you read these two letters that both Paul and James use Abraham as an illustration of true faith (Gal. 3:6–9; James 2:21–24). Abraham trusted God and lived out that trust by his actions.

A Closer Look—Philippians 2:12–13

To get a feel for the immediate context, read a few paragraphs before and after Philippians 2:12–13, our focal passage for this study. The word "therefore" in 2:12 points back to 2:1–11 (Jesus' humiliation-exaltation), a section we considered in Believing 7.

1. Why do you suppose that 2:12–13 comes immediately after 2:1–11? What is the relationship between these two sections?

Now look carefully at the text below and highlight significant words, important commands, purpose statements (e.g., "for . . ." in v. 13), crucial prepositional phrases (e.g., "with fear and trembling"), and so on. Use the margins to make comments, show connections, or ask questions.

¹²Therefore, my dear friends, as you have always obeyed—not only in my presence, but now much more in my absence—continue to work out your salvation with fear and trembling, ¹³for it is God who works in you to will and to act according to his good purpose.

BEHAVING 7—*Trusting and Acting*

Crossing the Bridge

As you cross the bridge from the ancient world to our world, what timeless theological principles do you see reflected in Philippians 2:12–13?

-

-

-

-

Partnering with God

C. S. Lewis comments on this whole issue of faith and works and Philippians 2:

> There are two parodies of the truth which different sets of Christians have, in the past, been accused by other Christians of believing. . . . One set were accused of saying "Good actions are all that matters. The best good action is charity. The best kind of charity is giving money. The best thing to give money to is the Church. So hand us over $10,000 and we will see you through." The answer to that nonsense, of course, would be that good actions done for that motive, done with the idea that Heaven can be bought, would not be good actions at all, but only commercial speculations.
>
> The other set were accused of saying, "Faith is all that matters. Consequently, if you have faith, it doesn't matter what you do. Sin away, my lad, and have a good time and Christ will see that it makes no difference in the end." The answer to that nonsense is that, if what you call your "faith" in Christ does not involve taking the slightest notice of what He says, then it is not Faith at all—not faith or trust in Him, but only intellectual acceptance of some theory about Him.
>
> The Bible really seems to clinch the matter when it puts the two things together into one amazing sentence. The first half is "Work out your own salvation with fear and trembling"—which looks as if everything depended on us and our good actions: but the second half goes on, "For it is God who works in you"—which looks as if God did everything and we nothing. . . . You see, we are now trying to understand, and to separate into water-tight compartments, what exactly God does and what man does when God and man are working together. And, of course, we begin by thinking it is like two men working together, so that you could say, "He did this bit and I

What Is Spiritual Formation?

Remember our definition of spiritual formation from the introduction?

> Spiritual formation is the process of allowing the Holy Spirit to conform us to the image of Jesus Christ.

Try to put into words why each element is vital:

- "process"

- "allowing"

- "Holy Spirit"

- "conform"

- "image of Jesus Christ"

No Verb for Faith?

Have you ever noticed that there is no English verb that corresponds to the English noun "faith"? We don't say "I faith God." We have to say "I believe in God." Do you think this language difference has contributed to our confusion about the relationship between faith and works? If so, how?

did that." But this way of thinking breaks down. God is not like that. He is inside you as well as outside. (*Mere Christianity*, 131–32)

God is at work within us, and he invites us to join him in the process. Make no mistake, spiritual growth is a lifelong process rather than a one-time event. In Philippians 3:1–14 and especially in verses 12–13 Paul talks about the process of spiritual growth. "I have not arrived," Paul says. But one thing he has learned to do—forget the past and press on toward the future that God has for him. The greatest danger as you take the journey is simply giving up or quitting. But be warned, spiritual formation is not optional. Everyone is being formed by someone or something. Because God has given us freedom, we can choose who or what will form us. Will it be the triune God who made us and loved us in Christ even while we were completely unlovable, or will it be forces opposed to God?

So What?

1. Has there ever been a time in your life when you knew that God was "at work in you"? How did you know?

2. Where and how is God at work in your life right now?

3. At this point in your life, what are the biggest obstacles to "working out your salvation" (i.e., allowing God to work in your life)?

4. What helps you "work out your salvation" without drifting into legalism? How do you *work out* your faith without that growing feeling that you have to *work for* certain things or God will no longer accept you?

5. As a community of believers, what specific things can you do to help individual members grasp and experience even more the reality of "working out your salvation"? What about the reality of God being at work in you?

6. What is the ultimate goal of spiritual growth anyway?

Faith?

There are three dimensions to biblical faith:

1. Intellectual faith, or belief (head), as in 1 John 4:1: "Dear friends, do not believe every spirit, but test the spirits to see whether they are from God."

2. Emotional faith, or trust (heart), as in 1 Peter 1:8: "Though you have not seen him, you love him; and even though you do not see him now, you believe in him and are filled with an inexpressible and glorious joy."

3. Volitional faith, or action (hands), as in Romans 1:5: "Through him and for his name's sake, we received grace and apostleship to call people from among all the Gentiles to the obedience that comes from faith."

Cross-References

Rom. 6; 12:1–2; 1 Cor. 6:9–11; 15:10; 2 Cor. 7:1; Phil. 3:12–14; 1 Thess. 1:3; 4:3–7; 2 Thess. 2:13–17; Heb. 10:9–14; 12:14; 13:20–21; James 2:14–26; 1 Peter 1:15–19; 2:1–3; 2 Peter 3:18; 1 John 3:2–3

For Deeper Study

Cloud, Henry, and John Townsend. *How People Grow.* Grand Rapids: Zondervan, 2001.
Foster, Richard J. *Celebration of Discipline.* 25th anniversary ed. San Francisco: HarperSanFrancisco, 2003.
Ortberg, John. *The Life You've Always Wanted.* Grand Rapids: Zondervan, 1997.

Jesus Loves Me, This I Know

Assurance

In the previous two parts of this chapter, we focused on the belief that salvation is by grace, through faith, for good works. We saw that this belief leads to the habit or practice of responding to God even as we trust him to work in our lives. Because God is at work in real and powerful ways, we respond to him by yielding our hearts to his leading. The Christian life cannot be reduced to willpower alone, simply gritting our teeth and trying to keep a list of laws. Neither is it entirely passive, where we sit back and "wait on God" to do it all. Genuine faith is a response to an encounter with the living God through Jesus Christ. Because we are in a new relationship, we will increasingly behave in ways that please our new Lord. Sometimes, however, our response isn't what it should be, and we begin to doubt our relationship. In Becoming 7 we turn our attention to the quality of being assured that God loves us and that we belong to God.

Do you know any insecure people? Often they are talkative, critical, even obnoxious as they clamor for other people's attention. Sometimes they are quiet, withdrawn, or sullen as they anticipate other people's disapproval. Insecure people crave affirmation and fear criticism. They will go to extremes—the latest fashion, a more expensive possession, "cynical humor," and the like—to find the love and acceptance they are so desperate for. Insecurity will stunt spiritual growth like nothing else because it eats away at the very foundation that God uses to build a life. Gordon Smith says it well.

Nothing is so fundamental to the Christian journey as knowing and feeling that we are loved. Nothing! . . . The only possible basis for growing in faith is the love of God—a love that we are sure and certain of. . . . We can find the wholeness for which we long only if we know, first, that we are loved. If this is taking a risk, it is a risk that

God will take. And there is no other foundation for spiritual growth and vitality than the confidence that we are loved. This is the gospel: God loves us. . . . Our greatest need is to know this truth and to anchor our lives to it, living in a profound inner confidence of God's love. (*Voice of Jesus*, 74, 78–79)

Insecurity is merely a symptom of a serious spiritual disease—an unwillingness to let God love us. For many of us the greatest challenge in life is accepting God's love and living securely and confidently like the child of God that we are. If you are a parent, can you imagine how you would feel if you found out one day that your children had been living in constant doubt that you really loved them? It's hard to imagine anything that would hurt more. If human parents hurt when they discover that their children don't feel their love, imagine how God must feel when we live in constant doubt about his love for us?

God desires that you have a profound confidence that you belong to him and a deep sense of security that he loves you as his precious child. Listen to God speak to your heart as you consider the following verses related to assurance:

My sheep listen to my voice; I know them, and they follow me. I give them eternal life, and they shall never perish; no one can snatch them out of my hand. My Father, who has given them to me, is greater than all; no one can snatch them out of my Father's hand. (John 10:27–29)

And hope does not disappoint us, because God has poured out his love into our hearts by the Holy Spirit, whom he has given us. You see, at just the right time, when we were still powerless, Christ died for the ungodly. Very rarely will anyone die for a righteous man, though for a good man someone might possibly dare to die. But God demonstrates his own love for us in this: While we were still sinners, Christ died for us. (Rom. 5:5–8)

Now it is God who makes both us and you stand firm in Christ. He anointed us, set his seal of ownership on us, and put his Spirit in our hearts as a deposit, guaranteeing what is to come. (2 Cor. 1:21–22)

And you also were included in Christ when you heard the word of truth, the gospel of your salvation. Having believed, you were marked in him with a seal, the promised Holy Spirit, who is a deposit guaranteeing our inheritance until the redemption of those who are God's possession—to the praise of his glory. (Eph. 1:13–14)

I pray that out of his glorious riches he may strengthen you with power through his Spirit in your inner being, so that Christ may

Amazing Love

If God is for us, who can ever be against us? Since God did not spare even his own Son but gave him up for us all, won't God, who gave us Christ, also give us everything else? Who dares accuse us whom God has chosen for his own? Will God? No! He is the one who has given us right standing with himself. Who then will condemn us? Will Christ Jesus? No, for he is the one who died for us and was raised to life for us and is sitting at the place of highest honor next to God, pleading for us. Can anything ever separate us from Christ's love? Does it mean he no longer loves us if we have trouble or calamity, or are persecuted, or are hungry or cold or in danger or threatened with death? . . . No, despite all these things, overwhelming victory is ours through Christ, who loved us. And I am convinced that nothing can ever separate us from his love. Death can't, and life can't. The angels can't, and the demons can't. Our fears for today, our worries about tomorrow, and even the powers of hell can't keep God's love away. Whether we are high above the sky or in the deepest ocean, nothing in all creation will ever be able to separate us from the love of God that is revealed in Christ Jesus our Lord.

—Romans 8:31–39 NLT

"The Spirit himself testifies with [to] our spirit"—This phrase teaches that the Holy Spirit produces the assurance that we deeply crave. The Spirit works in our hearts in ways that surpass words and go beyond logic to bring assurance that God loves us and we belong to him. The Holy Spirit is different from the spirit that condemns and enslaves us. God's Spirit is the one who gives us the inner certainty that God loves us like a perfect Father and that he will never stop loving us. As we realize once again that we belong to God, and that he has not forsaken us, we cry out, "*Abba, Father!*"

A Childlike Prayer
Take a few minutes and write a simple heart prayer to the Lord expressing how much the Spirit's assurance of God's love means to you.

dwell in your hearts through faith. And I pray that you, being rooted and established in love, may have power, together with all the saints, to grasp how wide and long and high and deep is the love of Christ, and to know this love that surpasses knowledge—that you may be filled to the measure of all the fullness of God. (Eph. 3:16–19)

In all my prayers for all of you, I always pray with joy because of your partnership in the gospel from the first day until now, being confident of this, that he who began a good work in you will carry it on to completion until the day of Christ Jesus. (Phil. 1:4–6)

That is why I am suffering as I am. Yet I am not ashamed, because I know whom I have believed, and am convinced that he is able to guard what I have entrusted to him for that day. (2 Tim. 1:12)

Therefore, brothers, since we have confidence to enter the Most Holy Place by the blood of Jesus, by a new and living way opened for us through the curtain, that is, his body, and since we have a great priest over the house of God, let us draw near to God with a sincere heart in full assurance of faith, having our hearts sprinkled to cleanse us from a guilty conscience and having our bodies washed with pure water. Let us hold unswervingly to the hope we profess, for he who promised is faithful. (Heb. 10:19–23)

Praise be to the God and Father of our Lord Jesus Christ! In his great mercy he has given us new birth into a living hope through the resurrection of Jesus Christ from the dead, and into an inheritance that can never perish, spoil or fade—kept in heaven for you, who through faith are shielded by God's power until the coming of the salvation that is ready to be revealed in the last time. (1 Peter 1:3–5)

How great is the love the Father has lavished on us, that we should be called children of God! And that is what we are! (1 John 3:1)

Dear children, let us not love with words or tongue but with actions and in truth. This then is how we know that we belong to the truth, and how we set our hearts at rest in his presence whenever our hearts condemn us. For God is greater than our hearts, and he knows everything. (1 John 3:18–20)

And this is the testimony: God has given us eternal life, and this life is in his Son. He who has the Son has life; he who does not have the Son of God does not have life. (1 John 5:11–12)

As you can tell from a brief look at only a few verses, assurance of salvation is based on what God has said (God's Word), what Jesus Christ has done (God's work), and what the Holy Spirit continues to do (God's witness). What God has promised and Christ has secured, the Spirit continues to confirm in our minds and hearts. The challenge for us is not to make ourselves feel less secure by ungodly living (the book of 1 John focuses on how a true believer will live).

A Closer Look—Romans 8:15–16

Take some time with Romans 8:15–16. Look for causes and effects, for important contrasts, and so on. Make your own notes in the margins as you dig into God's Word.

[15]For you did not receive a spirit [Holy Spirit] that makes you

a slave again to fear, but you received the Spirit of sonship.

And by him we cry, *"Abba,* Father." [16]The Spirit himself testi-

fies with [to] our spirit that we are God's children.

1. What roles does God play? What roles do we play?

2. Now read the surrounding context in your Bible (all of Romans 8). What do you see in this context that helps you understand what God is trying to say to you?

Crossing the Bridge

As you cross the bridge from the ancient world to our world, what timeless theological principles do you see reflected in Romans 8:15–16?

- When we become a Christian, we receive the Holy Spirit.

- The Holy Spirit does not promote fear and bondage but the freedom associated with being a child.

-

-

> **Does God Want Us to Doubt?**
> God wants his children to be sure that they belong to him, and does not want us to remain in doubt and uncertainty. So much so, that each of the three persons of the Trinity contributes to our assurance. The witness of God the Holy Spirit confirms the Word of God the Father concerning the work of God the Son. The three strong legs of this tripod make it very steady indeed.
>
> —John Stott,
> *Authentic Christianity,* 211

Cross-References

John 1:11–12; 5:24; 10:27–30; Rom. 4:16–21; 8:35–39; 2 Cor. 1:21–22; Gal. 4:4–7; Eph. 1:13–14; 3:12; 4:30; Phil. 1:3–6; 2 Tim. 1:12; Heb. 6:9–12; 10:19–23; 11:1; 1 Peter 1:3–5; 1 John 3:1, 18–24; 4:12–17; 5:11–12

For Deeper Study

Milne, Bruce. *Know the Truth.* Rev. ed. Downers Grove, IL: InterVarsity Press, 1998.

Ortberg, John. *Love Beyond Reason: Moving God's Love from Your Head to Your Heart.* Grand Rapids: Zondervan, 1998.

Smith, Gordon T. *The Voice of Jesus: Discernment, Prayer, and the Witness of the Spirit.* Downers Grove, IL: InterVarsity Press, 2003.

So What?

1. Assurance of salvation really amounts to being confident that God loves you and that you are his child. Many people believe in their heads that God loves them, but they do not feel it or sense it in their hearts. Why do you suppose this is the case?

2. What is the best advice you have ever received about accepting God's love?

3. Have you ever had negative experiences in church services where you were pressured to doubt your salvation? Now that you've had time to reflect on this experience, how do you feel about it? Was that experience helpful or harmful? Why?

4. Which of the assurance verses listed on pages 119–20 is most meaningful for you?

5. What are some things that we do as Christians to undermine our confidence that we belong to God?

6. What is one specific thing you can do this week to walk more securely and confidently in God's acceptance of you as his child?

A Promise Kept

Holy Spirit

The evangelist Billy Graham has written that human beings have two great spiritual needs—one is for forgiveness, the other is for goodness. God answered our first cry at Calvary by sending his Son to take our place so that we might receive forgiveness. God heard our second cry at Pentecost by giving us his Holy Spirit, who provides the power to live a transformed life (*The Holy Spirit*, 11–12). This study targets our belief that the Holy Spirit continues what Jesus began to do during his earthly ministry—transforming us from the inside out and empowering us to fulfill our mission in this world.

In Old Testament times, people were accustomed to God living in a tabernacle or large tent (Exod. 25:8–9) and then later in a temple (1 Kings 8:13). Of course, God has never been confined to an earthly building of any kind, but that's where he allowed people to experience his presence. Throughout the Old Testament, God promised a time when he would have a closer, more personal relationship with his people. He promised a time when he would pour out his own Spirit on his people and they would know him intimately.

> I will sprinkle clean water on you, and you will be clean; I will cleanse you from all your impurities and from all your idols. I will give you a new heart and put a new *spirit* in you; I will remove from you your heart of stone and give you a heart of flesh. And I will put my Spirit in you and move you to follow my decrees and be careful to keep my laws. (Ezek. 36:25–27)

> And afterward, I will pour out my Spirit on all people. Your sons and daughters will prophesy, your old men will dream dreams, your young men will see visions. Even on my servants, both men and women, I will pour out my Spirit in those days. (Joel 2:28–29)

God began to fulfill his promise in Jesus, who came in the power of the Spirit (see Mark 1:4–8; Luke 1:35; John 1:32–34). At the close of Jesus' earthly ministry, he assured his followers that the Father would soon fulfill his promise to send the Holy Spirit. The night before he was crucified, Jesus spent the evening teaching his disciples what to expect in the days and weeks

God's Real Temple

In the summer of 2000, Dr. Danny Hays and I led a study trip to Israel. Part of the trip included a visit to what remains of the temple in Jerusalem. At one point we took a break and sat on some old steps, one of the places where the experts told us Jesus most certainly walked. It was my turn to give a devotional thought to the group of students. As we looked around in awe at what appeared to be a holy place, I reminded them that the most holy thing they could see was not a certain wall or even the steps upon which we sat, but the people sitting next to them. Once God had a temple for his people. Now God's real temple is people, people indwelt by the Holy Spirit. As Paul says in 1 Corinthians 3:16, "Don't you know that you yourselves are God's temple and that God's Spirit lives in you [plural]?"

Pentecost?

Pentecost was originally an Old Testament festival that began on the fiftieth day after the beginning of Passover. During this celebration, people would give thanks to the Lord for the firstfruits of the early spring harvest (see Lev. 23:14–16). Christians now have the firstfruits of the Spirit as they wait for Jesus' second coming (Rom. 8:23). In the Christian calendar, Pentecost Sunday occurs on the seventh Sunday after Easter.

ahead. He washed their feet and taught them to serve. He gave them a new commandment and exhorted them to love. He spoke of a vine and its branches to illustrate how to bear spiritual fruit. He warned them to expect persecution from the world. He shared a meal with them and instituted the Lord's Supper. He assured them that lasting joy and peace would replace their short-term sorrow, and he prayed for them. His words of consolation also included instructions about the Holy Spirit. Look at what Jesus said about the Holy Spirit on that extraordinary night in the Upper Room.

> And I will ask the Father, and he will give you another Counselor to be with you forever—the Spirit of truth. The world cannot accept him, because it neither sees him nor knows him. But you know him, for he lives with you and will be in you. (John 14:16–17)

> All this I have spoken while still with you. But the Counselor, the Holy Spirit, whom the Father will send in my name, will teach you all things and will remind you of everything I have said to you. (John 14:25–26)

> When the Counselor comes, whom I will send to you from the Father, the Spirit of truth who goes out from the Father, he will testify about me. (John 15:26)

> But I tell you the truth: It is for your good that I am going away. Unless I go away, the Counselor will not come to you; but if I go, I will send him to you. When he comes, he will convict the world of guilt in regard to sin and righteousness and judgment: in regard to sin, because men do not believe in me; in regard to righteousness, because I am going to the Father, where you can see me no longer; and in regard to judgment, because the prince of this world now stands condemned. I have much more to say to you, more than you can now bear. But when he, the Spirit of truth, comes, he will guide you into all truth. He will not speak on his own; he will speak only what he hears, and he will tell you what is yet to come. He will bring glory to me by taking from what is mine and making it known to you. All that belongs to the Father is mine. That is why I said the Spirit will take from what is mine and make it known to you. (John 16:7–15)

After Jesus' resurrection he reminded his disciples of the soon-to-be-fulfilled promise: "Do not leave Jerusalem, but wait for the gift my Father promised, which you have heard me speak about. For John baptized with water, but in a few days you will be baptized with the Holy Spirit" (Acts 1:4–5). In the very next chapter of Acts, we read about God keeping his promise to pour out his Spirit and live among his people in a new way. The fulfillment of the promise occurs at Pentecost.

At Pentecost, God "got out of the building" so to speak and began to live in and among his people. When asked to explain what had just happened

BELIEVING 8—*Holy Spirit*

at Pentecost, the apostle Peter quotes Joel 2 (see page 123) as he explains that this mysterious event was God keeping his promise to live among his people in power. When people become Christ followers, God takes up residence within them in the person of the Holy Spirit. Paul summarizes:

> And you also were included in Christ when you heard the word of truth, the gospel of your salvation. Having believed, you were marked in him with a seal, the promised Holy Spirit, who is a deposit guaranteeing our inheritance until the redemption of those who are God's possession—to the praise of his glory. (Eph. 1:13–14)

Notice what is involved in this single, complex, life-changing event:

1. We hear the word of truth, the gospel.
2. We believe (faith).
3. We are included in Christ.
4. We are marked in Christ with a seal, the promised Holy Spirit (the deposit).

When we receive Christ, we receive the Holy Spirit. As Paul says in Romans 8:9: "And if anyone does not have the Spirit of Christ, he does not belong to Christ." Just as we are given new life by the Spirit at conversion (John 3:8), so we must continue to live by the Spirit (Gal. 3:2–3). The Spirit supplies boldness to witness, helps us say "no" to temptation, and produces spiritual fruit in our lives (e.g., love, joy, peace, patience). The Spirit assures us that we belong to Christ, makes us more like Christ, inspires true worship, convicts us of sin, guides us in making decisions, forms us into a community, and gifts us to minister to others. God actually lives in us by his Spirit. The Spirit guarantees that one day we will live in the very presence of God in the new heaven and new earth (see Rev. 21:3, 22; 22:3–4).

A Closer Look—John 14:16–17

Read our focal passage carefully. Identify the actions of different groups (Father, Son, Spirit, God's people, the world). Look for contrasts, reasons, promises, and relationships. Mark up the text below with your observations.

16And I will ask the Father, and he will give you another

Counselor to be with you forever—17the Spirit of truth.

The world cannot accept him, because it neither sees him

nor knows him. But you know him, for he lives with you

and will be in you.

"another"—There are two common Greek words for "another"—one meaning another of the same kind, and one meaning another of a different kind. In Galatians, Paul rebukes the Galatians for chasing after "another" (or a different) gospel (Gal. 1:6–7). In John 14, Jesus assures his disciples that although he is leaving them, he will send them "another" Counselor, another of the same kind, who will live in each of them and substitute for Jesus' physical presence.

"Counselor"—The Greek word, *paraklētos*, refers to "one who is called alongside to encourage or exhort." In ancient times the word carried legal overtones, as in a legal assistant or advocate (cf. 1 John 2:1). The NIV translation "Counselor" is adequate if we keep in mind a legal counselor rather than a marriage counselor or a mental-health counselor. The Holy Spirit is the one who pleads, convinces, and instructs us. He points us to what is real and true and stands beside us as our advocate, friend, and defender.

"world"—In the context of John 14:17, the "world" refers to people who are hostile to Jesus Christ and all that he stands for. The world hates Jesus and those who follow Jesus (John 15:18). By contrast, God loved the world and sent his Son to rescue the world (John 3:16).

SCRIPTURE NOTES

Cross-References

John 3:8; 1 Cor. 3:16; 6:19–20; 12:13; 2 Cor. 1:21–22; 6:16; Gal. 3:13–14; Eph. 2:21–22; Titus 3:4–7; 1 John 2:20, 27; 3:24; 4:13

For Deeper Study

Graham, Billy. *The Holy Spirit*. Dallas: Word, 1988.

Green, Michael. *I Believe in the Holy Spirit*. Rev. ed. Grand Rapids: Eerdmans, 2004.

Keener, Craig S. *Three Crucial Questions About the Holy Spirit*. Grand Rapids: Baker, 1996.

Morris, Leon. *The Gospel According to John*. Rev. ed. New International Commentary on the New Testament. Grand Rapids: Eerdmans, 1995.

Crossing the Bridge

What biblical principles do you see in John 14:16–17?

- "Counselor" indicates that the Holy Spirit is our advocate and defender.
- The Spirit is given by the Father to those who follow the Son.
-
-
-
-
-

So What?

1. Reread the passages from John 14–16 on page 124, and make a list of all that Jesus said the Holy Spirit would do.

2. How have you experienced the ministry of the Holy Spirit in your life?

3. How do you want the Spirit to work in your life in the near future?

4. Would you rather be an original disciple who had the privilege of walking and talking with Jesus or a disciple today who is permanently indwelt by the Holy Spirit? (Not that we have a choice, but it's fun to think about.)

5. Of all the biblical principles that you identified in "Crossing the Bridge," which is most applicable for you right now? Why?

Follow the Leader

Walking by the Spirit

God kept his promise and poured out his Spirit on his people at Pentecost. Since that time, God's Holy Spirit has dwelt within individual Christ followers. The Spirit supplies boldness, produces spiritual fruit, helps us resist temptation, assures us that we belong to Christ, inspires true worship, convicts us of sin, guides us into truth, forms us into a community, gifts us for ministry, and in many other ways continues the ministry of Jesus. We no longer have to meet God at the temple to experience his presence. God now lives among his people. This study focuses on our need to allow the Holy Spirit to carry out his ministry in our lives. God wants to be our source of strength and joy. He wants to deliver us from temptation and make us more like Christ, but we have to let him work in us. This calls us to the habit of walking by the Spirit.

You cannot become a Christian apart from the work of the Holy Spirit. The Christian life begins with the Spirit. Jesus himself said that "no one can enter the kingdom of God unless he is born of water and the Spirit" (John 3:5; cf. 3:8). Paul speaks of those who are "born by the power of the Spirit" (Gal. 4:29; cf. 4:6). Do you remember the critical time in your life when you were born of the Spirit?

The Christian life begins with the Holy Spirit, but sometimes we forget that the Christian life continues in just the same way. In his letter to the Galatians, Paul is dealing with a group of people who are dangerously close to forgetting that just as we are born of the Spirit, so also we go on living by the Spirit. Paul confronts them honestly about this deadly way of thinking: "Are you so foolish? After beginning with the Spirit, are you now trying to attain your goal by human effort [the flesh]?" (Gal. 3:3). Thank God that we don't bear the burden of finishing what he started. It's not that God begins our Christian life and then it's up to us to finish it. No, not at all. We have the privilege of relying on the Spirit to complete what he began in our lives. What a relief! Just as we trusted

In Ephesians 4:30 Paul says, "And do not grieve the Holy Spirit of God, with whom you were sealed for the day of redemption." "Grieve" refers to a hurt or sorrow felt by God. When we sin, we normally feel guilt or shame. When we sin, God grieves. Our sin hurts God's heart. (See how the word is used in Matt. 17:23; 19:22; 26:37; John 16:20; 21:17; 2 Cor. 2:4; 1 Thess. 4:13.)

THE POWER OF WORDS

"live"—This command in 5:16 could be translated "walk" (NASB). We often speak of our Christian "walk" as a metaphor for our way of life, and that's how the word is used here. Paul is commanding the Galatians (and us) to choose a certain way of life that relies on the Spirit.

"flesh"—In this context, the "flesh" is not referring to the human body. Our physical bodies can be used for good or bad, but the Bible doesn't teach that they are innately evil. The "flesh" here refers to human nature in its fallen state (NIV: "sinful nature"). Flesh stands in opposition to Spirit just as autonomous, self-reliant human beings stand against God. When we follow the "flesh," we pretend to be our own god and act as if the one, true God did not exist. People who follow the flesh will either become focused on religious rules resulting in legalism (the Galatians) or abandon rules altogether resulting in libertinism (the Corinthians). The flesh represents our tendency to do life apart from God.

"keep in step with"—This is a military expression that portrays soldiers marching in a straight line. The Spirit leads and we follow. It takes discipline and concentration to pay attention to the Spirit above the competing voices and follow in his footsteps. We do not have to achieve grace; we are commanded to follow.

God's work in Christ to give us new life in the first place, so we can trust God's work through the Holy Spirit to grow us up and make us more like Jesus. The question is, how do we let the Spirit do his important work?

Our focal text is from Galatians 5:16 and 25, but we can't understand the specific verses without seeing the larger picture. Paul brought the good news of Christ to the Galatians and later learned that they were being hounded by false teachers. The false teachers were saying to the Galatians: "If you want to be first-rate Christians, full-fledged Christians, real Christians, then you need to supplement your new faith in Christ with a few important Jewish rules such as eating particular foods, observing special days, and submitting to certain religious rituals, especially circumcision." You can imagine how confused these Galatians had become. Why do you suppose new converts often feel attracted to rule-oriented religion?

- It just feels safer.
- It offers tangible, measurable results.
- They hope the additional rules will help them conquer the flesh.
- It's much less complicated, and they prefer to keep it simple.
-
-

Paul calls this "Jesus-plus" message a "different gospel" since it brings spiritual slavery rather than real freedom—"I am astonished that you are so quickly deserting the one who called you by the grace of Christ and are turning to a different gospel—which is really no gospel at all" (Gal. 1:6–7a). Paul writes his letter to the Galatians to condemn the false teaching and to persuade these new believers to continue in the true gospel—trusting Christ and following the Holy Spirit. Here is how Paul's line of argument flows through the last part of Galatians.

➡ Jesus set you free from the obligation to keep the law. (5:1, 13a)
➡ But you are not free in Christ to indulge your flesh. (5:13b, 15, 26)
➡ Rather, you are free to love one another. (5:13b)
➡ Why is love so important? Because love fulfills the law (the reason you were attracted to this false teaching in the first place; it seemed more spiritual). (5:14)
➡ OK, so love fulfills the law. How do we love?
➡ You follow the Holy Spirit, who creates love! (5:16–18, 25)
➡ We need specifics. Show us what a flesh life looks like in contrast to a Spirit life.
  - When you are indulging the flesh, your life will look more like 5:19–21.
  - When you are following the Spirit, your life will look more like 5:22–24 and 6:1–10.

There is a wealth of spiritual truth in Galatians 5:1–6:10. Take a moment and read this passage if you haven't already. Now do something creative. Use the space below to summarize in your own words Paul's line of argument explained on the previous page.

Pastoral Wisdom

F. B. Meyer, an influential pastor and Bible teacher who ministered in the late nineteenth and early twentieth centuries, once said:

The Spirit of the Lord Jesus Christ is *present* in all true Christians. He is *prominent* in some, and He is *pre-eminent*, alas, in only a few.

—Lyle Dorsett,
Seeking the Secret Place, 18–19

A Closer Look—Galatians 5:16, 25

In light of the context, look carefully at the two verses below. Underline each command. Double underline the basis of each command (if there is one). Circle repeated words. Bracket off results or promises. Read about significant words in the sidebar on page 128. Make other observations and ask questions in the margins.

SCRIPTURE NOTES

¹⁶So I say, live [walk] by the Spirit, and you will not gratify

the desires of the sinful nature [flesh]. . . . ²⁵Since we live by

the Spirit, let us keep in step with the Spirit.

Crossing the Bridge

What biblical principles do you see in Galatians 5:16, 25 or any other place in the larger context of Galatians 5–6? The first two are done for you.

- The law shows us what is right (i.e., God's standard), but only Christ can set us free and only the Spirit can give us the power to live up to that standard.

- In "following the leader" I am both passive ("led by" in 5:18) and active ("walk by" in 5:16).

Cross-References

Do you ever look up any of these references? See the references from Believing 8 and others throughout this section.

For Deeper Study

Fung, Ronald Y. K. *The Epistle to the Galatians.* New International Commentary on the New Testament. Grand Rapids: Eerdmans, 1988.

Hansen, G. Walter. *Galatians.* IVP New Testament Commentary. Downers Grove, IL: InterVarsity Press, 1994.

Packer, J. I. *Keep in Step with the Spirit.* Grand Rapids: Revell, 1984.

Stott, John R. W. *Baptism and Fullness: The Work of the Holy Spirit Today.* Downers Grove, IL: InterVarsity Press, 1975.

•

•

•

•

So What?

1. What do you think about the idea of "grieving the Spirit"? From the examples surrounding Ephesians 4:30, what are the most common ways that you grieve the Spirit?

2. Read "Grammar Matters!" in the sidebar. If the promise is absolute when the condition is met (i.e., *if* we follow the Spirit, we will *never* gratify the flesh), then what should our strategy be for conquering the flesh? How does this compare to our typical strategy?

3. How is following the Spirit more adventuresome and daring than trying to keep the law?

4. How do you discern the Spirit's "voice" in order to march in a straight line behind him?

5. What specific things do you need to do or avoid doing in order to stay more in step with the Spirit?

What's Growing On?

Fruit of the Spirit

When we begin a relationship with Jesus Christ, we are in reality "born of the Spirit" (John 3:5–8). God wants our new life to continue the same way it began. He wants us to "walk by the Spirit." It's not that God begins our Christian life and then it's up to us to finish it. He wants us to rely on him to complete what he started. We do this by refusing to reduce our new relationship to nothing more than a set of religious rules. The law has no power to tame the flesh (our inclination to do life apart from God). But when we discern the Spirit's voice and follow him, it will be totally and absolutely impossible for us to gratify the flesh at the same time. As we grow in the habit of staying in step with the Spirit, our lives begin to resemble Christ himself. This Christ "look" is best portrayed by the fruit-of-the-Spirit list in Galatians 5, the focus of Becoming 8.

As we talked about in Believing 8, when people become Christ followers, God takes up residence within them in the person of the Holy Spirit. Paul summarizes:

> And you also were included in Christ when you heard the word of truth, the gospel of your salvation. Having believed, you were marked in him with a seal, the promised Holy Spirit, who is a deposit guaranteeing our inheritance until the redemption of those who are God's possession—to the praise of his glory. (Eph. 1:13–14)

This complex, life-changing event includes hearing the gospel, believing, being included in Christ, and being sealed with the Holy Spirit. (Sometimes the New Testament uses the phrase "baptism in the Spirit" to refer to what happens to a person at conversion.) At the end of that same letter to the

Think about the following characteristics of Paul's command in Ephesians 5:18 to "be filled":

* Present tense—ongoing or repeated filling
* Imperative mood—a command to be carrried out
* Passive voice—allowing God to fill us
* Plural—not just for "super-Christians" but for all obedient believers

With these things in mind, how would you translate the second part of Ephesians 5:18?

"Keep on . . .

Ephesians, however, Paul speaks about another ministry of the Holy Spirit—the fullness of the Spirit.

> Be very careful, then, how you live—*not* as unwise *but* as wise, making the most of every opportunity, because the days are evil.
>
> Therefore do *not* be foolish, *but* understand what the Lord's will is.
>
> Do *not* get drunk on wine, which leads to debauchery. *Instead, be filled with the Spirit.* Speak to one another with psalms, hymns and spiritual songs. Sing and make music in your heart to the Lord, always giving thanks to God the Father for everything, in the name of our Lord Jesus Christ. Submit to one another out of reverence for Christ. (Eph. 5:15–21)

As Paul describes how Christians should live, he uses three statements, each having two parts—"do not do this, . . . but do that." The third statement tells us not to get drunk on wine, which leads to out-of-control, destructive living, but to be filled with the Spirit. A person who is filled with the Spirit will be a person of worship, community, joy, gratitude, and relational humility.

Being filled with the Spirit (Eph. 5) is really about the same thing as walking by the Spirit (Gal. 5). It's not that you get more of the Spirit, but that the Spirit gets more of you. To get a better sense of what it means to live a Spirit-filled life, we need to look at the context of Galatians 5:22–24, our focal passage for this study.

We see from Galatians 5:16–21 that the Holy Spirit and the flesh have declared war on each other. These two opposing powers produce in their followers a distinct character or way of life. What is allowed to reign in a person's heart will eventually work its way out to that person's behavior and will be plain for all to see. Paul makes it clear that the flesh (sinful nature) results in a chaotic existence (better described as death than life) that can be divided into several categories: (1) *sexual sins*—sexual immorality, impurity, debauchery; (2) *false religion*—idolatry, witchcraft; (3) *sins against the community*—hatred, discord, jealousy, fits of rage, selfish ambition, dissensions, factions, envy; and (4) *pagan living*—drunkenness, orgies, and the like. Paul warns that "those who live like this will not inherit the kingdom of God" (5:21). In contrast, the Spirit life looks totally different.

A Closer Look—Galatians 5:22–24

Look carefully at the verses on the next page. Mark your observations (lists, explanations, results, etc.). Read about significant words in the text below the verses. Think also about how this virtue list differs radically from the vice list that precedes it.

²²But the fruit of the Spirit is love, joy, peace, patience,

kindness, goodness, faithfulness, ²³gentleness and self-

control. Against such things there is no law. ²⁴Those who

belong to Christ Jesus have crucified the sinful nature with

its passions and desires.

1. Paul may be "holding the mirror up to the Galatians" by contrasting the sins against the community that occur in the middle of the flesh list (Gal. 5:20–21) with the fruit of the Spirit. Can you match vices and virtues that appear to be opposites?

Hatred	Love
Discord	Joy
Jealousy	Peace
Fits of rage	Patience
Selfish ambition	Kindness
Dissensions	Goodness
Factions	Faithfulness
Envy	Gentleness
	Self-control

2. Consider the meaning of each term in the fruit list. Think honestly about your life and relationships and how they match up to what the Spirit desires.

- **Love** (*agapē*)—Love heads the list of qualities because it is a reflection of the very nature of God. All other virtues flow out of love, which is much more than tolerance or sentiment. Love is a commitment to do what God thinks is best for another person. See 1 Corinthians 13 for a full description.
- **Joy** (*chara*)—More than human happiness, joy is a settled excitement that results from healthy relationships, including our relationship with God. Joy originates, not from immediate circumstances or passing pleasures, but from the Spirit.
- **Peace** (*eirēnē*)—More than the absence of conflict, peace is a deep contentment and wholeness that comes from harmonious relationships.

Lights Without Electricity

Imagine visiting a town at night that appears to have no lights, no televisions—not even alarm clocks. And then imagine learning that the town's power supply is virtually infinite, but that no one in the town had thought to turn any of their electrical appliances on. Wouldn't that town seem like a silly place to you? Yet the Church is all too often like that town. God has given us the power of His Spirit to fulfill His mission in the world, yet few Christians have even begun to depend on His power.

—Craig Keener,
Three Crucial Questions, 17

"fruit of the Spirit"—The "works" of the flesh are plural, reflecting the chaotic and disjointed nature of evil. In contrast, we do not read about the "works" of the Spirit, but about the "fruit" of the Spirit. "Fruit" is singular, reflecting the unity and harmony of God's work in our lives. Fruit is something that the Spirit grows or produces in us as we cooperate with him. It represents character qualities born out in our attitudes and actions. To put it another way, the fruit of the Spirit is a picture of what it means to be like Jesus.

"have crucified the sinful nature [flesh]"— This past-tense statement probably refers to our conversion and baptism, when we publicly identified with Christ. A common baptism confession goes like this:

Do you turn to Christ?
  I turn to Christ.
Do you repent of your sins?
  I repent of my sins.
Do you renounce evil?
  I renounce evil.

This is when we initially said "no" to evil and "yes" to Christ. As the flesh and the Spirit battle, we must return to the promise we made at our baptism. Having been buried and raised with Christ (Gal. 2:20), we continue to crucify the flesh. Our lifelong commitment is not to negotiate with the flesh, but to continuously crucify the flesh as a part of walking by the Spirit.

- **Patience** (*makrothymia*)—The word is also translated "long-suffering." It refers to the patient enduring of some wrong without taking revenge or responding in anger. This generosity of heart calls us to bear with one another when irritated or provoked rather than to retaliate.
- **Kindness** (*chrēstotēs*)—Kindness is a sweet and gracious disposition toward others.
- **Goodness** (*agathōsynē*)—This is the outworking of the attitude of kindness in doing good to others in practical and generous ways.
- **Faithfulness** (*pistis*)—Faithfulness refers to the quality of loyalty and trustworthiness in relationships. When we are faithful, rather than being fickle or foolish, we can be counted on to keep our commitments.
- **Gentleness** (*prautēs*)—The word also is translated "meekness." As the opposite of arrogance and selfish ambition, gentleness refers to a humble submission to the Spirit that leads us to consider the needs and hurts of others ahead of our personal desires. Only a secure strength can act patiently and mildly toward others.
- **Self-control** (*ekkrateia*)—This is the opposite of self-indulgence. This quality refers to the strength and discipline (that comes from the Spirit) to control our passions and resist temptation.

No wonder Paul says that "against such things there is no law" (5:23). When we try to live up to a list of religious rules, we fail because we are relying on our own human ability. When we allow the Spirit to fill us and lead us, the Spirit produces a certain kind of life. The Spirit-led life is not a violation of the law. Rather, those who walk by the Spirit fulfill the law.

So What?

1. Has the Holy Spirit been over- or underemphasized in your church experience? (Some might want to say that the Spirit has been properly emphasized.) What do you think you have missed if you have not been getting balanced teaching on the Spirit?

2. How would you translate Ephesians 5:18 (see sidebar on page 132)? Why is this verse crucial to a proper understanding of the Holy Spirit?

3. As you think about the fruit list, which ones most characterize your life? Which ones least characterize your life?

4. Again, thinking about the fruit list, when has the Spirit been allowed to produce his fruit in greatest abundance in your life? In other words, in what kind of life seasons or situations are you walking by the Spirit most faithfully?

5. What are some practical things that help you to crucify the flesh?

6. Chapter 8 has focused on the Holy Spirit. What has been most helpful and meaningful to you from this chapter?

Don't Pull Out the Nails

The first great secret of holiness lies in the degree and the decisiveness of our repentance. If besetting sins persistently plague us, it is either because we have never truly repented, or because, having repented, we have not maintained our repentance. It is as if, having nailed our old nature to the cross, we keep wistfully returning to the scene of its execution. We begin to fondle it, to caress it, to long for its release, even to try to take it down again from the cross. We need to learn to leave it there. When some jealous, or proud, or malicious, or impure thought invades our mind we must kick it out at once. It is fatal to begin to examine it and consider whether we are going to give in to it or not. We have declared war on it; we are not going to resume negotiations. . . . We have crucified the flesh; we are never going to [with]draw the nails.

—John Stott,
Message of Galatians, 151–52

For Deeper Study

Fung, Ronald Y. K. *The Epistle to the Galatians.* New International Commentary on the New Testament. Grand Rapids: Eerdmans, 1988.

Hansen, G. Walter. *Galatians.* IVP New Testament Commentary. Downers Grove, IL: InterVarsity Press, 1994.

Stott, John R. W. *Baptism and Fullness: The Work of the Holy Spirit Today.* Downers Grove, IL: InterVarsity Press, 1975.

Stott, John R. W. *The Message of Galatians.* The Bible Speaks Today. Downers Grove, IL: InterVarsity Press, 1968.

The People of God

The Church

Are you trying to live the Christian life all by yourself?

We cannot live the Christian life in isolation, like some religious Robinson Crusoe. Membership in the church is not an optional extra. The fact is, we cannot be fully Christian without belonging to the church. As we study the New Testament we find that to be a Christian is to be "in Christ," and that this means being a member of a new society of which Christ is the living Head—the church. The New Testament knows nothing of unattached Christians. Consider the matter in a more mundane way. What would we think of a man who said that he wanted to be a soldier but insisted that he could be a perfectly good one without joining the army? An unattached soldier is nonsense—and so is the notion of a solitary Christian. (Shelley, *Theology for Ordinary People*, 146)

The necessity of community is not something that comes naturally for Christians living in an individualistic culture. Some of us have to learn the hard way. When we pull away from church or when we neglect church, we are the ones who suffer. We grow cold and loveless. Relating to God means relating to the people of God. We need each other. In Believing 9 we will focus on the church: Christ's body and bride, the Spirit's temple, and the Father's family.

In the New Testament, the word for "church" is *ekklēsia*, meaning "called out ones." This important word describes a community of people from every tribe, language, people, and nation that belongs to Jesus Christ, the head of the church. Most of the time the word *ekklēsia* refers to a *local community* of those who profess allegiance to Christ and gather regularly for the purpose of worship and fellowship (e.g., "the church in Corinth" or "the church in Philippi"). At other times, the word depicts the *universal church*—all believers across the world and throughout the ages (e.g., Eph. 5:25: "Christ loved the church and gave himself up for her"). One thing is certain, an *ekklēsia* (church) was not just a civic association or religious club, but a community called out by God. As Bruce Shelley puts it, "The church . . . is more than an aggregation—people who have chosen to come together. It is a congregation, a people called together" by God (*Theology for Ordinary People*, 139). The church is not merely an organization or an institution providing religious programs or a place to find help in your individual walk with God. The church is not a building; it is people. The church is a spiritual organism, a living reality that draws its life from the very life of the triune God, the perfect community.

To grasp the New Testament concept of church, we need to look beyond the word *ekklēsia* to the central images or word pictures of the church. There are many such images (one writer lists over a hundred), but we will spend a few minutes with four main ones. I could tell you about these, but it will mean more to you if you discover them for yourself. Look up the key verses for each image and write a brief summary of what each image signifies and why it is important for our understanding of church.

- Body of Christ (Rom. 12:4–5; 1 Cor. 12:12–27; Eph. 3:6; 5:23; Col. 1:18–24; 2:19; 3:15)

- Bride of Christ (Eph. 5:25, 27, 31–32; Rev. 19:7; 21:2; 22:17)

- Temple of the Spirit (1 Cor. 3:16–17; 2 Cor. 6:16; Eph. 2:21–22; Heb. 3:6; 10:21; 1 Peter 2:5; Rev. 21:2–3, 10–22)

- Household/Family of God (Gal. 6:10; Eph. 2:19; 3:15; 1 Tim. 3:15; Heb. 2:11; 1 Peter 4:17)

A Closer Look—1 Peter 2:4–10

Our focal passage is one of the most profound passages on the church in the New Testament. Take time to dig deep into this text. Mark up the passage with your observations. Look for important words, lists, contrasts, comparisons, purpose statements, significant phrases, figures of speech, conjunctions, emotional terms, time indicators, and so on. Before you can know what the Bible means, you need to observe what it says.

A Mosaic

Community is like a large mosaic. Each little piece seems so insignificant. One piece is bright red, another cold blue or dull green, another warm purple, another sharp yellow, another shining gold. Some look precious, others ordinary. Some look valuable, others worthless. Some look gaudy, others delicate. As individual stones, we can do little with them except compare them and judge their beauty and value. When, however, all these little stones are brought together in one big mosaic portraying the face of Christ, who would ever question the importance of any one of them? If one of them, even the least spectacular one, is missing, the face is incomplete. Together in the one mosaic, each little stone is indispensable and makes a unique contribution to the glory of God. That's community, a fellowship of little people who together make God visible in the world.

—Henri Nouwen,
Only Necessary Thing, 124

Life Without Church?

The virtuous soul that is alone . . . is like a burning coal that is alone. It will grow colder rather than hotter.

—St. John of the Cross,
quoted in Philip Yancey, *Church*, 23

⁴As you come to him, the living Stone—rejected by men but chosen by God and precious to him—⁵you also, like living stones, are being built into a spiritual house to be a holy priesthood, offering spiritual sacrifices acceptable to God through Jesus Christ. ⁶For in Scripture it says: "See, I lay a stone in Zion, a chosen and precious cornerstone, and the one who trusts in him will never be put to shame" [Isa. 28:16]. . . . ⁹But you are a chosen people, a royal priesthood, a holy nation, a people belonging to God, that you may declare the praises of him who called you out of darkness into his wonderful light. ¹⁰Once you were not a people, but now you are the people of God; once you had not received mercy, but now you have received mercy.

THE POWER OF WORDS

"the living Stone"—Jesus was compared to food in 2:3, but now he is identified as a stone—the stone that the human builders rejected and crucified. To God, however, this "Stone" is precious. Rather than being a lifeless thing like a normal rock, Jesus has been raised from the dead and is the "living Stone" (see 1 Peter 1:18–21).

"a spiritual house"—The Rock (Jesus) is building a new house, a spiritual temple where God will live. This house is made up of "living stones"—people who belong to Jesus. As living stones connected to the living Stone, we are part of a community where God himself lives through his Spirit.

"spiritual sacrifices"—This term refers to the offering of ourselves to God (cf. Rom. 12:1). We offer to God our praise (cf. Heb. 13:15–16) and our service (e.g., Phil. 4:18). God desires both our words of worship and our acts of service. Also, spiritual sacrifices (those that honor the Holy Spirit) should be offered with the proper motives and attitudes.

Crossing the Bridge

What biblical principles do you see in 1 Peter 2:4–10?

- Since we experience biblical community "through Jesus Christ" (v. 5), we need to see Christ as the true source of genuine community and not try to generate community around any other source.

-

-

-

So What?

1. Do you really think church is essential to the Christian life? Why or why not?

2. What place does church hold right now in your life? Do you need to make any changes?

3. Many of us have grown up in a culture that prizes the individual and emphasizes self-sufficiency above the community. How has this individualistic culture affected your approach to church?

4. Which of the four central images of the church is most meaningful to you at this time in your life? Why?

5. What small step could your church take to encourage genuine community?

6. How could you participate in making this happen?

"cornerstone"—In an ancient building the cornerstone was a very large and costly stone that anchored the entire structure. This massive foundation stone bound together different rows of stones and provided strength and precision for the rest of the building. As a spiritual house or temple, God's people are built upon Jesus, the precious cornerstone (see Eph. 2:20).

The Future of the Church

The future of the church depends on whether it develops true community. We can get by for a while on size, skilled communication, and programs to meet every need, but unless we sense that we belong to each other, with masks off, the vibrant church of today will become the powerless church of tomorrow.

—Larry Crabb in foreword to Randy Frazee, *Connecting Church*, 13

Cross-References

Matt. 16:13–20; 18:15–17; Acts 1–2, 10–11; Rom. 12:3–8; 1 Cor. 1:10–17; 3:1–17; 12:12–27; 14:1–40; 2 Cor. 6:16; Eph. 1:22–23; 2:11–22; 3:6–11; 4:3–16; 5:23, 25–27, 31–32; Col. 1:15–24; 2:19; 1 Tim. 3:1–13, 15; Titus 1:5–9; Heb. 3:6; 10:19–25; Rev. 2–3, 19:1–9; 21:1–27; 22:17

For Deeper Study

Banks, Robert. *Paul's Idea of Community*. Rev. ed. Peabody, MA: Hendrickson, 1994.

Gibbs, Eddie. *ChurchNext*. Downers Grove, IL: InterVarsity Press, 2000.

Stanley, Andy, and Bill Willits. *Creating Community*. Sisters, OR: Multnomah, 2004.

Wilson, Jonathon R. *Why Church Matters: Worship, Ministry, and Mission in Practice*. Grand Rapids: Baker, 2006.

Yancey, Philip. *Church: Why Bother?* Grand Rapids: Zondervan, 1998.

Personal Glory or Kingdom Greatness?

Serving

Although our culture says that life should revolve around the individual, God reminds us that when we enter a relationship with Jesus Christ, we become part of Christ's body, the church. We cannot experience the Christian life in isolation from other Christians. We are a "chosen people, a royal priesthood, a holy nation, a people belonging to God, that [we] may declare the praises of him who called [us] out of darkness into his wonderful light" (1 Peter 2:9). Once we were a bunch of scattered loners, but now, by the grace of Jesus Christ, we are the people of God. We have been called together (or congregated) in Christ. We don't have to go it alone. We get to experience life in community, and this life flows from the triune God, the perfect community.

Being a member of the people of God is not only a privilege; it is also a responsibility. In Behaving 9 we will concentrate on our need to serve each other. As members of Christ's body, we are called to meet each other's needs through acts of practical service. As "living stones" in God's spiritual house, we offer spiritual sacrifices—not only to praise God but also to minister to other members of God's family.

Rusty Stevens, a ministry leader who lives in Virginia Beach, Virginia, tells this story.

As I feverishly pushed the lawn mower around our yard, I wondered if I'd finish before dinner. Mikey, our 6-year-old, walked up and, without even asking, stepped in front of me and placed his hands on the mower handle. Knowing that he wanted to help me, I quit pushing.

The mower quickly slowed to a stop. Chuckling inwardly at his struggles, I resisted the urge to say, "Get out of here kid. You're in my way," and said instead, "Here, son. I'll help you." As I resumed pushing, I bowed my back and leaned forward, and walked spread-legged to avoid colliding with Mikey. The grass cutting continued, but more slowly, and less efficiently than before, because Mikey was "helping" me.

Suddenly, tears came to my eyes as it hit me: *This is the way my heavenly Father allows me to "help" him build his kingdom!* I pictured my heavenly Father at work seeking, saving, and transforming people, and there I was, with my weak hands "helping." My Father *could* do the work by himself, but he doesn't. He chooses to stoop gracefully to allow me to co-labor with him. Why? For *my* sake, because he wants me to have the privilege of ministering with him. (Larson, *Illustrations*, 153)

Although God allows us to "help" him by allowing us to serve others, we sometimes have trouble accepting service as a divine opportunity. The first disciples had the same struggle, as we will see from the focal passage in Mark 10. Sadly, in the mirror of their lust for power, selfish ambition, inflated egos, and spiritual ignorance, we sometimes see our own reflection.

A Closer Look—Mark 10:35–45

One of the best ways to get inside a story is to ask the typical story questions: Who? What? When? Where? Why? and How? Find Mark 10:35–45 in your Bible. In the space below answer the questions about Jesus' teaching on kingdom greatness. One of the boxes has been done for you. Once you've experienced a story by looking at it from all angles, you will never again be content to "skim" a story (e.g., notice the contrast between vv. 35 and 45).

"the cup . . . the baptism"—Jesus mentions drinking a cup and being baptized with a baptism in Mark 10:38. These words are metaphors for suffering. In Gethsemane Jesus would pray, "Take this cup from me" (Mark 14:36) when referring to his impending suffering and death. He also refers to these events as his "baptism" (Luke 12:50). When Jesus asks James and John if they can drink the cup and undergo the baptism, they flippantly answer, "We can." The truth is that they have not yet connected greatness in the kingdom with suffering. Glory and suffering go together (Rom. 8:17).

"ransom"—In ancient writings this term referred to the payment made to free a slave or a prisoner (i.e., the price of release). Ransom is tied to the cost of life and freedom. Jesus gave his life "in place of" or "instead of" the many. Jesus substituted himself for the many. We should have died because of our sins, but he died in our place. Here we see the ultimate form of service.

WHO?	WHAT?

chart continued on next page…

WHEN?	WHERE?
	James and John approach Jesus, apart from the other disciples, in order to get something (v. 35).
	James and John desire to sit on Jesus' "right and left" when he comes into his glory (vv. 37, 40). Check out Mark 15:27, the only other place where these same words occur in Mark.
	The places of honor (v. 40).
	The ten other disciples got close enough to hear Jesus' response (v. 41).
	Jesus called everybody together (v. 42).
	The Son of Man (Jesus) comes to human beings (v. 45). Notice how Jesus' "approach" to serve as a ransom (v. 45) differs radically from the approach of James and John to secure worldly glory (v. 35).
WHY?	**HOW?**

A Real Servant?

A wise person once said that you will know whether you are a servant by how you respond when you are treated like one.

Crossing the Bridge

What biblical principles do you see in Mark 10:35–45? Below are two examples to get you started.

- We should beware of uncritically embracing pagan models of greatness.

- Jesus was willing to oppose popular expectations about servanthood in order to be a true servant. The religious culture of that time expected a Messiah that would conquer the Romans and establish an earthly kingdom. Jesus came as a "suffering Messiah" for the purpose of establishing an eternal kingdom.

-

-

-

-

-

Since service strongly relates to our motives, Richard Foster's distinction between "self-righteous service" and "true service" is insightful and convicting (*Celebration of Discipline*, 128–30).

- *Self-righteous service* comes through human effort. It expends immense amounts of energy calculating and scheming about how to render service. *True service*, however, comes from our relationship with God, from divine promptings and urgings.
- *Self-righteous service* is impressed with the "big deal," whereas *true service* finds it almost impossible to distinguish the small from the large service.
- *Self-righteous service* requires external rewards, but *true service* is content with remaining hidden from the spotlight.
- *Self-righteous service* is concerned with results and becomes bitter if expectations are not met, while *true service* is free from the need to measure results.
- *Self-righteous service* picks and chooses whom to serve, favoring the high and powerful. *True service*, on the other hand, does not discriminate in its ministry.
- *Self-righteous service* is affected by moods and whims, serving only when the feelings are present. *True service* knows it can't depend on feelings and ministers faithfully because there is a need.
- *Self-righteous service* is temporary, resting easy after the service has been performed. By contrast, *true service* is a lifestyle and mind-set.
- *Self-righteous service* centers on glorifying the individual and spoils community. *True service* builds community by genuinely caring for the needs of others.

So What?

1. How does the story in Mark 10:35–45 affect your understanding of and commitment to being a servant?

The Ministry of the Towel

Read John 13:1–17. As you read, imagine that Jesus is approaching you with a basin of water and a towel. Your heart begins to beat faster as you realize that he plans to wash your feet. In the space below write down what might go through your head as Jesus stoops to serve you.

Rights Left Behind

When we choose to be a servant, we give up the right to be in charge. There is great freedom in this. . . . When we choose to be a servant, we surrender the right to decide who and when we will serve. We become available and vulnerable.

—Richard Foster,
Celebration of Discipline, 132

Cross-References

Matt. 20:20–28; John 13:1–17; Acts 6:1–6; Rom. 12:11; 1 Cor. 12:5; 2 Cor. 4:5; 13:4; Gal. 1:10; 6:2; Eph. 4:12; Phil. 2:1–11; Col. 3:23–24; James 1:27; 1 Peter 4:10

For Deeper Study

Berding, Kenneth A. *What Are Spiritual Gifts? Rethinking the Conventional View.* Grand Rapids: Kregel, 2006.

Bugbee, Bruce. *What You Do Best in the Body of Christ.* Rev. and exp. Grand Rapids: Zondervan, 2005.

Garland, David E. *Mark.* NIV Application Commentary. Grand Rapids: Zondervan, 1996.

2. Why do you suppose that Jesus chooses service to define greatness? In other words, why does service seem like such a big deal to God?

3. As members of his community, Christ desires that we serve each other. He allows us to "help" him by serving each other. In your life, what are the great obstacles to service?

4. Which type of "self-righteous service" mentioned by Foster is the biggest trap for you? Why?

5. What inspires and motivates you to serve?

6. What are some specific ways that we can serve each other? What are some ways we can serve people outside our community?

It's Not About Me

Humility

> "Nowhere in the Great Tradition of Christianity before the twentieth century can one find the uniquely modern phenomenon of 'churchless Christianity'" (Olson, *Mosaic*, 292). Since we weren't made for "church-less Christianity," we will suffer more than we can imagine if we neglect God's provision of church. We were created for community, and if we really believe that we are relationally connected to other members of the body of Christ and are part of the same family, then we will make each other a priority. We will serve each other. John Ortberg is on tar-get when he says that "authentic community is characterized perhaps more than anything else by mutual servanthood and submission" (*Life You've Always Wanted*, 111). Service does something to us that nothing else can do. It frees us from the prison of being absorbed and preoc-cupied with ourselves. This self-forgetfulness can also be described as humility. In Becoming 9 we will see how the habit of service produces in us the quality of humility.

It may seem strange, but getting a handle on humility begins by under-standing its opposite—pride. "Pride is spiritual cancer," writes C. S. Lewis in his remarkable chapter on "The Great Sin" in *Mere Christianity* (pages 109–14). Pride, he says, is "the essential vice, the utmost evil." It leads to every other sin because it is the "complete anti-God state of mind."

How do you know if you are a proud person? Lewis offers a reliable test—the more pride we have, the more we will dislike it in other people because pride is "essentially competitive." Pride is like playing a game in which we invent the rules and rig the outcome so that we always win. Anyone who has more influence or ability or money or brains (or anything) than I have, is my enemy. Pride sets out to defeat the rival through an all-out competition.

Subject or Object?

How many times in the story does the Pharisee appear as the subject in his own statements?

Notice that the only time the tax collector mentions himself, he is the object.

The worst part is that pride can creep right into the center of our religious lives. Lewis warns, "Whenever we find that our religious life is making us feel that we are good—above all, that we are better than someone else—I think we may be sure that we are being acted on, not by God, but by the devil." The very bottom of the deep, dark pride pit is where "you look down on others so much that you don't care what they think of you." Their opinion is worthless because we are so far above them that they are worthless in our eyes.

In our focal story from Luke 18, Jesus confronts those "who were confident of their own righteousness and looked down on everybody else" (v. 9). In a religious competition between the Pharisee and the tax collector, everyone would expect the Pharisee to win, but God uses a different scorecard. "In God," Lewis says, "you come up against something which is in every respect immeasurably superior to yourself. Unless you know God as that—and, therefore, know yourself as nothing in comparison—you do not know God at all."

A Closer Look—Luke 18:9–14

Locate the parable of the Pharisee and the tax collector in your Bible. Ask the standard story questions like you did with our last story: Who? What? When? Where? Why? and How? Write your answers in the boxes below. There are no shortcuts to reading a story closely. It's hard work and it takes time, but the rewards are great.

WHO?	WHAT?

WHEN?	WHERE?

WHY?	HOW?

Crossing the Bridge

Two men go up to the temple to pray—one a highly respected religious leader and the other a much-despised traitor and cheat. But something unexpected happens during this prayer time, and the story takes a surprising turn at the end. Now that you have studied the story carefully, what do you see as the main points or principles of the story?

"Pharisee"—The Pharisees were the most pious group of people in Jewish society. They tried to interpret the law carefully and went beyond others in applying it to every aspect of life. In their interpretation, they gave priority to the traditions of men. The people greatly respected the Pharisees as religious leaders and experts.

"tax collector"—Tax collectors were likely the most hated group in Jewish society. Since they collaborated with the occupying pagan government (Rome), they were seen as traitors. They often collected too much tax and became wealthy at the expense of the people.

"righteousness . . . evildoers . . . justified"—These words don't appear to have anything in common in English, but they do in Greek. They are all built on the same root (-δικ). What difference does this make? Jesus tells the parable to confront those who are confident of their own "righteousness" and look down on everybody else. The Pharisee boasts that he is not an "evildoer" or "unjust" like other people. But because the Pharisee's heart is full of pride, the humble tax collector is the one who goes home "justified." The Pharisee goes home unjustified (i.e., as an evildoer), the very condition he claimed did not apply to him. This little wordplay sums up the whole story.

- Religious activity such as prayer, fasting, and tithing does not guarantee that a person is closely connected to God.

- When it comes to right standing before God, the standard is not a human one, but a heavenly one.

-

-

-

Cultivating Humility

Often stories in the Gospels send a message by how they are connected to surrounding stories. The story that comes right before our focal story is about an unjust judge and a widow (Luke 18:1–8). That story highlights the widow's persevering faith and ends with a question: "When the Son of Man comes, will he find faith on the earth?" You can almost hear the Pharisees answer, "Well, of course he will find faith on the earth, and he will find it among us, the Pharisees. We are the faithful ones." Jesus then tells the parable of 18:9–14 to show that there are some surprises when it comes to who has faith and who doesn't. God puts a premium on humility. Notice also the episode that follows our focal story. As people bring their children to Jesus, he uses this as an object lesson of real faith—"anyone who will not receive the kingdom of God like a little child will never enter it" (Luke 18:17). The simple, humble, sincere faith of a child stands alongside the humble faith of a repentant tax collector and in contrast to the proud "faith" of the overconfident and arrogant Pharisee.

The problem then is pride, and the solution is humility. Take a look at how one author defines humility in the sidebar on page 149. Humility is having a healthy, realistic view of ourselves, of others, and of God. It is realizing that God is God and we are not. Humility means that we focus on others rather than on ourselves, not that we draw even more attention to ourselves by pretending to be worthless nobodies. So how do we cultivate humility? The first step is to admit that we are proud (not a small step). Foster suggests the next step:

> More than any other single way, the grace of humility is worked into our lives through . . . service. Humility, as we all know, is one of those virtues that is never gained by seeking it. The more we pursue it the more distant it becomes. To think we have it is sure evidence that we don't. Therefore, most of us assume there is nothing we can do to gain this prized Christian virtue, and so we do nothing. But there *is* something we can do. . . . Service is the most conducive to the growth of humility. When we set out on a

consciously chosen course of action that accents the good of others and is, for the most part, a hidden work, a deep change occurs in our spirits. (*Celebration of Discipline*, 130)

So What?

1. Most of us have a lot to learn about humility. What have you learned about pride and humility in Becoming 9? How can you begin to apply what you have learned?

2. Do you tend toward "low pride" (pretending that you are nothing) or "high pride" (pretending that you are everything)? Explain your answer.

3. Can you think of some ways that we use religious activity to cover up a prideful heart? (Remember that pious practices are not inherently evil since the tax collector also goes to the temple to pray.)

4. As you think about times in your life when you have served, how does the practice of service seem to change you?

Humility: What It Is and Isn't

Humility is not about convincing ourselves—or others—that we are unattractive or incompetent. It is not about "beating ourselves up" or trying to make ourselves nothing. If God wanted to make us nothing, he could have done it.

Humility has to do with a submitted willingness. It involves a healthy self-forgetfulness. We will know we have begun to make progress in humility when we find that we get so enabled by the Holy Spirit to live in the moment that we cease to be preoccupied with ourselves, one way or the other. When we are with others, we are truly *with* them, not wondering how they can be of benefit to us. . . . Humility involves . . . the realization that the universe does not revolve around us. . . . Humility is the freedom to stop trying to be what we're not, or pretending to be what we're not and accepting our "appropriate smallness."

—John Ortberg,
Life You've Always Wanted, 102–3

Cross-References

Deut. 8:11–18; 2 Chron. 7:14; Pss. 18:27; 147:6; Prov. 3:34; Isa. 57:15; 66:2; Matt. 23:12; Luke 14:11; Phil. 2:1–11; James 4:10; 1 Peter 5:5–7

For Deeper Study

Bock, Darrell L. *Luke.* NIV Application Commentary. Grand Rapids: Zondervan, 1996.

Foster, Richard J. *Celebration of Discipline.* 25th anniversary ed. San Francisco: HarperSanFrancisco, 2003.

Lewis, C. S. *Mere Christianity.* New York: Macmillan, 1952.

5. It appears that we often compartmentalize service in unfair ways. For example, the people who set up chairs for a worship service or wash dishes after a church gathering are real servants, while those who pray for the gathering or write the drama script to be used during the worship time are not usually thought of as servants. Do you think we have trouble seeing the many dimensions of service? Why or why not?

6. What are some ways that you think God might be calling you to serve your community at this point in your life?

Trying Versus Training

Transformation

Let's review for a minute. We have said that spiritual formation is the process of allowing the Holy Spirit to conform us to the image of Jesus Christ (see Behaving 7, page 115). God often uses resources such as *Experiencing God's Story of Life and Hope* to help the process along. We won't always obey God just because we ought to. We will obey God because in him alone we find life and hope. In our heart of hearts we want to respond to God's gift of life with a deeper and stronger love for him. God desires this kind of whole-life response that connects believing, behaving, and becoming, all of which are rooted and grounded in God's kingdom story as revealed in Scripture (see the Believing column of the overview, pages 16–17). In Ephesians 3:14–21 Paul prays that his readers might understand and experience God's great story. Read his prayer slowly and pray it for yourself.

> When I think of the wisdom and scope of God's plan, I fall to my knees and pray to the Father, the Creator of everything in heaven and on earth. I pray that from his glorious, unlimited resources he will give you mighty inner strength through his Holy Spirit. And I pray that Christ will be more and more at home in your hearts as you trust in him. May your roots go down deep into the soil of God's marvelous love. And may you have the power to understand, as all God's people should, how wide, how long, how high, and how deep his love really is. May you experience the love of Christ, though it is so great you will never fully understand it. Then you will be filled with the fullness of life and power that comes from God. Now glory be to God! By his mighty power at work within us, he is able to accomplish infinitely more than we would ever dare to ask or hope. May he be given glory in the church and in Christ Jesus forever and ever through endless ages. Amen. (NLT)

When it comes to transformation, artists and athletes have it right. They grasp what the rest of us sometimes miss—that growth is an intentional process. Whether it be voice lessons or choir rehearsal, soccer practice or

"God's mercy"—The underlying Greek term translated "mercy" by the NIV is plural—"mercies." Romans 1–11 spells out the many ways that God has poured out his mercies on us. The command to "offer" our bodies to God is based upon these mercies. We don't obey in order to earn mercy; rather, God's mercy is the basis for our obedience—the only appropriate response to God's grace (cf. Rom. 6:13, 16, 19).

"living sacrifices, holy and pleasing"—The sacrifices we offer to God are described in three ways: living, holy, and pleasing to God. Unlike sacrificial animals that were put to death, we go on living. As sacrifices, our lives should be set apart and pleasing to God. This is true worship.

"spiritual act of worship"—Offering ourselves as sacrifices to God is equated with "spiritual worship." The adjective translated "spiritual" (*logikos*) probably refers to the idea of "informed" or "deliberate." Again, unlike sacrificial animals that did not understand what was happening to them, we give ourselves to God willingly and with full understanding. The word "worship" (KJV: "service") should be understood broadly to include all of life and not just a time of praise.

SCRIPTURE NOTES

volleyball drills, artists and athletes understand that growth takes time and effort. They are not just trying harder; they have entered a life of training. John Ortberg describes the difference between *trying* and *training*:

> For much of my life, when I heard messages about following Jesus, I thought in terms of *trying hard* to be like him. So after hearing . . . a sermon on patience on Sunday, I would wake up on Monday morning determined to be a more patient person. Have you ever tried hard to be patient with a three-year-old? I have—and it generally didn't work any better than would my trying hard to run a marathon for which I had not trained. I would end up exhausted and defeated. . . . Spiritual transformation is not a matter of trying harder, but of training wisely. (*Life You've Always Wanted*, 47)

What would you say are some differences between trying and training?

A Closer Look—Romans 12:1–2

One of the key texts on transformation is found at the beginning of Romans 12. Our focal passage serves as the bridge between the more "theological" section of Romans 1–11 and the more "practical" section of Romans 12–16 (see "Make It Practical" on page 154). Take time to dig deep into God's Word. Circle the verbs, put a box around the key nouns, and note the lists and what they describe. Identify the contrasts, the conjunctions, the explanations of how and why, along with result statements. Read "The Power of Words" to the left. Don't miss a thing. This is one juicy passage!

[1]Therefore, I urge you, brothers [and sisters], in view of God's mercy, to offer your bodies as living sacrifices, holy and pleasing to God—this is your spiritual act of worship. [2]Do not conform any longer to the pattern of this world, but be transformed by the renewing of your mind. Then you will be able to test and approve what God's will is—his good, pleasing and perfect will.

Crossing the Bridge

Remember, a theological principle is a present-tense statement of a timeless truth that applies equally well to the biblical audience and to us. What theological principles do you see in Romans 12:1–2?

- Our worship is a response to God's mercy. Mercy always comes before obedience.

- Worship includes offering both the body and the mind to God. The Christian life is not just a mental game. If we do not offer our bodies, we do not worship.

-

-

-

Spiritual Disciplines

Transformation takes time and effort. I am not suggesting that we can earn salvation by good works but encouraging us to admit that a genuine experience of grace produces fruit (see again Behaving 7). Sometimes we use grace as an excuse *not* to offer our bodies or to resist conformity to the world or to renew our minds, unless we are put "on the spot" to be like Jesus. Dallas Willard illustrates what usually happens when we try to act like Christ only when we are put to the test:

> Think of certain young people who idolize an outstanding baseball player. . . . When they are playing in a baseball game, they all try to behave exactly as their favorite baseball star does. . . . These young people try anything and everything their idol does, hoping to be like him—they buy the type of shoes the star wears, the same glove he uses, the same bat. . . . Will they succeed in performing like the star, though? . . . We know that they won't succeed if all they do is try to be like him in the game . . . and we all understand why. The star performer himself didn't achieve his excellence by trying to behave in a certain way *only during the game.* Instead, he chose an overall life preparation of mind and body, pouring all his energies into that total preparation, to provide a foundation in the body's automatic responses and strength for his conscious efforts during the game. . . . A baseball player who expects to excel in the game without adequate exercise of his body is no more ridiculous than the Christian who hopes to be able to act in the manner of Christ when put to the test without the appropriate exercise in godly living. . . . We cannot behave "on the spot" as he [Christ] did and

"conform . . . to the pattern of this world"—To be conformed is to be forced into a mold or pattern (see also Becoming 3). This "world" (literally, "age") refers to the ungodly mindset and behavior of those who do not know God (cf. Eph. 2:1–3). The present-tense command suggests that we need to repeatedly refuse to let this "age" mold or shape us.

"be transformed"—The negative command not to conform is replaced with the positive command to be transformed. This word is used to describe Jesus' transfiguration (Matt. 17:2; Mark 9:2) and here refers to the ongoing renewal and change that Jesus brings through his Spirit (see 2 Cor. 3:7–18).

A Transformed Person

A disciplined [or mature] person is someone who can do the right *thing* at the right *time* in the right *way* with the right spirit [or *motive*].

—John Ortberg,
Life You've Always Wanted, 54

Do you need to make an important decision or evaluate a recent action? Use these four questions to evaluate your decision:

- Is this the right thing to do?
- Is the timing right?
- Am I doing this in the right way?
- Am I doing this for the right reason?

taught if in the rest of our time we live as everybody else does. . . . Our efforts to take control *at that moment* will fail so uniformly and so ingloriously that the whole project of following Christ will appear ridiculous to the watching world. (*Spirit of the Disciplines*, 3–7)

We need to enter a life of training and discipline, much like an athlete or an artist. We need to do more than try hard when the pressure is on; we need to train ourselves to be godly as a way of life (1 Tim. 4:7–8). *Spiritual disciplines* are habits or practices that place us before God so that he can transform us. They are tools in God's hands that he uses to shape and mold us to be more like Jesus. Spiritual disciplines include prayer, submission, study, meditation, service, confession, solitude, and silence, just to name a few. Almost any activity can become a training exercise. Spiritual disciplines take us beyond merely trying harder; they enable us to train wisely.

So What?

1. If we are convinced that consistent training is more valuable to spiritual transformation than sporadic trying, why do we so often settle for trying?

2. Both the "body" and the "mind" are mentioned in Romans 12:1–2. Do we associate spiritual growth more with the mind or the body? What do we lose if we neglect the other aspect?

3. As you think about John Ortberg's definition of "A Transformed Person" given on page 153, which one of the four questions do you struggle with the most?

4. Which spiritual discipline has God used to grow you?

5. As you think about Romans 12:1–2, trying versus training, and spiritual disciplines, what specific step do you believe God wants you to take to "test and approve" his good, pleasing, and perfect will?

Cross-References

John 15:4–8; Rom. 6:12–14; 8:29; 1 Cor. 10:31; 2 Cor. 3:7–18; 4:16; Gal. 2:20; 4:19; Eph. 4:22–24; Phil. 1:6; 2:12–13; 3:7–14; Col. 3:10; 1 Tim. 4:7; James 1:2–4; 1 Peter 2:2–3

For Deeper Study

Cloud, Henry, and John Townsend. *How People Grow*. Grand Rapids: Zondervan, 2001.

Moo, Douglas J. *Romans*. NIV Application Commentary. Grand Rapids: Zondervan, 2000.

Willard, Dallas. *Renovation of the Heart*. Colorado Springs: NavPress, 2002.

Willard, Dallas. *The Spirit of the Disciplines*. San Francisco: HarperSanFrancisco, 1988.

Only One Thing Matters

Praying

God's mercy draws us to worship him. True worship occurs when we offer ourselves, bodies and all, to God. Rather than being shaped by ways of the world, we are transformed by God himself. When it comes to transformation, artists and athletes correctly realize that change occurs not just by trying harder in certain on-the-spot situations, but by training consistently over time. Training involves spiritual disciplines or practices that place us before God so that he has time and space to do his transforming work. Prayer is one such spiritual discipline, and many people consider prayer to be the central discipline because it lies at the heart of our relationship with God. Referring to Jesus' statement to a busy and worried woman in Luke 10:42, Henri Nouwen writes, "Prayer is the center of the Christian life. *It is the only necessary thing.* . . . It is living with God here and now" (*Only Necessary Thing*, 25). Prayer is more than just talking to God; prayer is communion with God that comes out of a heart that has experienced the love of God. In Behaving 10 we turn our attention to what Jesus taught his first disciples about communing with the Father.

About 1490 two young friends, Albrecht Dürer and Franz Knigstein, were struggling young artists. Since both were poor, they worked to support themselves while they studied art. Work took so much of their time and advancement was slow. Finally, they reached an agreement: they would draw lots, and one of them would work to support both of them while the other would study art. Albrecht won and began to study, while Franz worked at hard labor to support them. They agreed that when Albrecht was successful he would support Franz who would then study art.

Albrecht went off to the cities of Europe to study. As the world now knows, he had not only talent but genius. When he had attained success, he went back to keep his bargain with Franz. But Albrecht soon discovered the enormous price his friend had paid. For as Franz worked at hard manual labor to support his friend, his fingers had become stiff and twisted. His slender, sensitive hands had been ruined for life. He could no longer execute the delicate brush strokes necessary to fine painting. Though his artistic dreams could never be fully realized, he was not embittered but rather rejoiced in his friend's success.

One day Dürer came upon his friend unexpectedly and found him kneeling with his gnarled hands intertwined in prayer, quietly praying for the success of his friend although he himself could no longer be an artist. Albrecht Dürer, the great genius, hurriedly sketched the folded hands of his faithful friend and later completed a truly great masterpiece known as "The Praying Hands." (Gray, *Stories for the Heart*, 261)

"One day Jesus was praying in a certain place. When he finished, one of his disciples said to him, 'Lord, teach us to pray.'" (Luke 11:1). His response has traditionally been called "The Lord's Prayer," although Jesus himself intended it as a model prayer for his followers.

A Closer Look—Matthew 6:9–13

1. Before teaching the disciples how to pray, Jesus teaches them how *not* to pray. Read Matthew 6:5–8 and complete the following chart on what to avoid in prayer.

	"Do not be like the hypocrites" (Matt. 6:5–6)	"Do not keep on babbling like pagans" (Matt. 6:7–8)
Why should we not pray in this way?		
What is the result of praying in this way?		

chart continued on next page...

"hallowed"—Since there is no contemporary verb for "holy" in English, we use this older word (we could start using the word *holified*). God is holy and defines what it means to be holy. People and things are holy when they are closely related to God (see Becoming 3). We are not praying here that God will become holy but that we would treat God as holy.

"kingdom"—This term refers to God's rule or reign. The kingdom of God has broken into this world with the coming of Christ and will one day be made known fully at the second coming of Christ. To pray for God's kingdom to come is to (1) pray that more people would come under God's rule now and (2) that God would soon finish the project (e.g., Rev. 22:20).

"daily bread"—Most people in Jesus' day were paid at the end of each day. As a result, this is a prayer for God to meet our basic needs, including physical needs, one day at a time. This is a request for needs, not wants. Also, the word "today" reminds us that the present day, rather than the future, should be our focus. God wants us to depend on him continually for our needs.

	"Do not be like the hypocrites" (Matt. 6:5–6)	"Do not keep on babbling like pagans" (Matt. 6:7–8)
How should we pray instead?		

Look at the prayer from Matthew 6:9–13. Looking especially at the pronouns, identify the pattern or organization to the prayer.

⁹Our Father in heaven,

hallowed be your name,

¹⁰your kingdom come,

your will be done

on earth as it is in heaven.

¹¹Give us today our daily bread.

¹²Forgive us our debts, as we also have forgiven our

debtors.

¹³And lead us not into temptation, but deliver us from

the evil one.

THE POWER OF WORDS

"temptation"—This word can be used to refer to a temptation to sin or to a trial or test. Since God does not tempt people to do evil or sin (James 1:13), this is probably a request for God not to lead us into a trial that will be too strong for us and surely result in a fall. This is the idea in Mark 14:38 and Galatians 6:1. In other words, we are praying for spiritual protection.

2. Did you notice that the first three requests are God centered? Write a short paragraph about what you think this part of the prayer means (i.e., God's name, kingdom, and will).

BEHAVING 10—*Praying*

3. The second set of three requests is centered on human beings. One of these requests deals with forgiveness. Read Matthew 6:12, 14–15. What do these verses teach about forgiveness?

Crossing the Bridge

What theological principles do you see in Matthew 6:9–13?

-
-
-
-

Now that you have briefly studied The Lord's Prayer, write a paraphrase of the prayer (i.e., rephrase the prayer in your own words). Make it personal by imagining that Jesus himself is instructing you today about how to pray.

So What?

1. What part of Jesus' teachings on prayer in Matthew 6 do you most need to apply to your life right now?

2. What keeps you from praying more?

Unanswered Prayer?

For our sins, Jesus suffered beneath the burden of unanswered prayer.

—Andrew Murray, *With Christ*, 211

What Do You Think?

What do you think C. S. Lewis meant when he said that in prayer "we must lay before Him what is in us, not what ought to be in us" (*Letters to Malcolm*, 22)?

Cross-References

1 Sam. 12:23; 2 Chron. 7:14; Neh. 1:4–11; Ps. 143:1; Isa. 56:7; Dan. 6:10; Jonah 2:1–9; Matt. 6:5–15; Mark 1:35; 14:32–39; Luke 5:16; 11:1; John 17; Acts 1:14; 2:42; 13:3; 16:25; Rom. 8:26; Eph. 3:14–21; Phil. 1:3–4; Col. 4:2; 1 Thess. 5:17; James 5:13–16; 1 Peter 3:12; 4:7

For Deeper Study

Foster, Richard J. *Prayer: Finding the Heart's True Home.* San Francisco: HarperSanFrancisco, 1992.

Hybels, Bill. *Too Busy Not to Pray.* Rev. and exp. Downers Grove, IL: InterVarsity Press, 1998.

Lewis, C. S. *Letters to Malcolm Chiefly on Prayer.* New York: Harcourt, 1964.

Nouwen, Henri J. M. *The Only Necessary Thing.* New York: Crossroad, 1999.

Yancey, Philip. *Prayer: Does It Make Any Difference?* Grand Rapids: Zondervan, 2006.

3. What has helped you to stay consistent when it comes to prayer?

4. Read "Prayer Paralysis?" in the sidebar on page 159. Are you paralyzed by thinking that you have to get your life straightened out before you can pray? How can you begin to pray "what is in you," not what ought to be in you?

5. How has God changed you through prayer? Give some examples.

Practicing His Presence

Peace

Our heavenly Father has determined to make us more like the Son. To accomplish his transforming work, the Father often encourages spiritual practices such as prayer. In prayer we open our hearts to God so that he may give us life and hope. Prayer involves a transfer of trust from ourselves—our abilities, our resources, our knowledge, our possessions—to God. Instead of wallowing in worry and fear, we let God know what we are thinking and feeling. As we pray, we begin to change. Sometimes gradually and at other times quickly, the chaos and turmoil and confusion give way to God's peace, a peace that is too wonderful to comprehend fully and too magnificent to achieve. In Becoming 10 we will look at how God's peace comes as the fruit of transformation and prayer.

There is always something to worry about. During the week I was writing this study on peace, I discovered that someone had stolen our credit card and charged over $1,000. Would we lose the money, or would the bank reimburse us? My wife Judy had recently traveled to Louisiana with a group of students to help with disaster relief. She returned with an extremely bad case of poison ivy. Even with all the medication, the itching was painful and caused her to lose sleep. Would this stuff ever go away? During a recent fall break, one of our students had been killed in a car wreck. I did not know the student, but what could I say to those who knew him well? Recently a "friend" made some choices that were both professionally inappropriate and personally disrespectful to me. How should I respond to this situation? Sometimes when it rains, it pours. What is on your worry list?

Although we will always have opportunities to worry, God promises peace when we abide in him through prayer. Have you ever deliberately practiced God's presence by consciously thinking about him throughout the day?

Prayer with Thanksgiving Produces Peace

Matthew Henry is a well-known Bible commentator. One day he was robbed and that evening made the following entry in his diary:

Let me be thankful—first, because I was never robbed before; second, because although they took my wallet they did not take my life; third, because although they took my all, it was not much; and fourth, because it was I who was robbed, not I who robbed.

—Alice Gray,
Stories for the Heart, 86

SCRIPTURE NOTES

A Blessing of Peace

The LORD bless you and keep you; the LORD make his face shine upon you and be gracious to you; the LORD turn his face toward you and give you peace.

—Numbers 6:24–26

Frank Laubach (1884–1970), a missionary to the Philippines, knew what it meant to pray without ceasing.

As I analyze myself I find several things happening to me as a result of these two months of strenuous effort to keep the Lord in mind every minute. This concentration upon God is strenuous, *but everything else has ceased to be so.* I think more clearly, I forget less frequently. Things which I did with a strain before, I now do easily and with no effort whatever. I worry about nothing, and lose no sleep. I walk on air a good part of the time. Even the mirror reveals a new light in my eyes and face. I no longer feel in a hurry about anything. . . . Each minute I meet calmly as though it were not important. Nothing can go wrong excepting one thing. That is that God may slip from my mind if I do not keep on my guard. If He is there, the universe is with me. My task is simple and clear. (Laubach, *Letters*, May 24, 1930)

Whether or not you subscribe to Laubach's approach, one thing is obvious—if we prayed more, we would worry less and experience more of God's peace. Let's go the Scriptures.

A Closer Look—Philippians 4:6–7

In the passage below locate any commands, contrasts, results, promises, figures of speech, descriptions ("which"), and locations ("in").

[6]Do not be anxious about anything, but in everything, by prayer and petition, with thanksgiving, present your requests to God.

[7]And the peace of God, which transcends all understanding, will guard your hearts and your minds in Christ Jesus.

1. What do the words "anything" and "everything" indicate?

2. Identify the different words for prayer used in this passage.

3. What attitude should accompany our prayers? Why is this important?

4. What is the major contrast in verse 6?

5. What is the promise contained in verse 7?

6. What kind of work does the "peace of God" do in our lives?

7. Read Philippians 4:1–9. How does the surrounding context help you understand 4:6–7?

"anxious"—When used positively, this word can refer to a healthy concern for people, such as Timothy's concern for the Philippians (Phil. 2:20) or the concern Christians should have for each other (1 Cor. 12:25). Negatively, however, the word signifies fearful, unproductive worry. Jesus clearly told us not to worry (Matt. 6:25–34; Luke 12:22–34). In a similar way, Paul commands us not to be worried or anxious about anything.

"peace"—Since "peace" stands in contrast to anxiety or worry in this context, it indicates a deep sense of well-being, wholeness, and inner contentment supplied by God. The "God of peace" (Phil. 4:9) promises the "peace of God" when we choose to pray instead of worry.

"transcends all understanding"—God's peace goes completely beyond all human ways of comprehending or understanding life. Human reasoning alone leads only to doubt and anxiety. God's ways are higher than our ways and we can trust him and experience his peace even when we don't fully understand everything.

"guard"—This is a military word used of soldiers standing guard over a city and protecting it (see 2 Cor. 11:32). Since a Roman garrison was stationed in Philippi, the readers could easily understand this figure of speech. The word picture shows that God's peace will surround and protect our hearts and thoughts against destructive worry.

Crossing the Bridge

What timeless truths do you see in Philippians 4:6–7?

-

-

-

As you looked closely at Philippians 4:6–7, did you notice that God's peace comes when we pray, not when we get a certain answer to prayer? Long before we get the answer we want or even before we get an answer at all, peace comes through the very act of praying. In prayer we transfer our trust from ourselves and our ability to control life to God and his resources.

As we cast our cares on him, worries are replaced with a calmness of heart and mind. We are *either* worrying *or* praying; never both at the same time. In Matthew 6:25–33, Jesus puts it all in perspective by saying something like, "If you want to worry, worry about something important. Stop stressing over the little stuff like clothes and money, and seek God's kingdom and his righteousness."

So What?

1. From your closer look at Philippians 4:6–7, what is most encouraging and helpful to you?

2. What are the top five things you could be worried about right now in your life?

BECOMING 10—*Peace*

3. How does praying "with thanksgiving" change your outlook and perspective about the situation you are praying about?

4. If prayer leads to peace and we are not experiencing peace, what do we need to change about the way we pray?

Now it's time to stop answering discussion questions and actually pray about what is making you anxious, fearful, angry, or frustrated. Don't just think about these things; really pray about them.

Cross-References

Num. 6:24–26; Pss. 1:1–3; 23:1–6; 34:14; 46:1–11; 119:165; Prov. 14:30; Isa. 26:3; 41:10; Matt. 6:25–34; 11:28; John 14:27; 16:33; Rom. 8:6; 14:17; 15:13; Gal. 5:22; Phil. 4:8–13; Col. 3:15

For Deeper Study

Baillie, John. *The Diary of Private Prayer.* New York: Scribner, 1949.

Brother Lawrence. *The Practice of the Presence of God.* Reprint. New Kensington, PA: Whitaker House, 1982.

Fee, Gordon D. *Paul's Letter to the Philippians.* New International Commentary on the New Testament. Grand Rapids: Eerdmans, 1995.

Laubach, Frank. *Letters by a Modern Mystic.* Westwood, NJ: Revell, 1958.

Why Are We Still Here?

Mission

Have you ever wondered why God doesn't take us to heaven immediately after we become followers of Jesus Christ? Why does he allow us to stay in this world where Satan prowls around like a lion looking for someone to devour (1 Peter 5:8)? God's kingdom story helps us answer that question.

God leaves us on earth even after we have been rescued because he is a missionary God and he wants us to join him in the mission. God has granted us the privilege of living and sharing his kingdom story. We endure the attacks of Satan, the pitfalls of sin, and the many dangers of a fallen world because there are people who need to be rescued.

Think about it this way. Let's suppose that your family lives in an area that is vulnerable to flash flooding. On one occasion torrential rains cause a sudden flood. You are pulled to safety, but in the confusion you mistakenly think that your entire family also has been rescued. Later you realize that your daughter is still trapped in the backyard tree house. You're safe, but someone you deeply love remains in danger. Wouldn't you do everything in your power to bring about a rescue? You bet your life you would!

When it comes to rescuing people from Satan and sin and death, the passion to save comes straight from God's own heart.

> The call of God is to share in his own mission in the world. First, he sent his Son. Then he sent his Spirit. Now he sends his church, that is, us. He sends us out by his Spirit into his world to announce his Son's salvation. He worked through his Son to achieve it; he works through us to make it known. (Stott, *Authentic Christianity,* 316)

After Jesus had been put to death on the cross and raised from the dead, he met with his followers to give them instructions about what to do after he ascended to the Father. Here is what he told them:

All authority in heaven and on earth has been given to me. Therefore go and make disciples of all nations, baptizing them in the name of the Father and of the Son and of the Holy Spirit, and teaching them to obey everything I have commanded you. And surely I am with you always, to the very end of the age. (Matt. 28:18–20)

This is what is written: The Christ will suffer and rise from the dead on the third day, and repentance and forgiveness of sins will be preached in his name to all nations, beginning at Jerusalem. You are witnesses of these things. (Luke 24:46–48)

Peace be with you! As the Father has sent me, I am sending you. (John 20:21)

It's hard to believe that Jesus entrusted the entire mission to such a common, ordinary bunch of people, but the fact is these "average Joes" radically changed their world. They were completely convinced that God's great story had reached its climax in Jesus, the Rescuer or Savior. They believed that God himself had become a man in order to save them from their sins. They weren't just trying to live by a higher law or advocating a new religion. They had found life in the person of Jesus Christ, risen from the dead! How can you keep quiet when you find life? When you know the answer, how can you keep it a secret? You cannot remain silent and passive and apathetic when you experience grace and forgiveness, freedom and hope. When you know what it means to be fully known and fully loved by your Creator, it leads you to worship. We talk about whatever or whomever we worship. We want others to find life and bow down beside us as we worship the Life Giver, to whom be the glory forever and ever. That's our mission.

A Closer Look—Matthew 28:18–20

Our focal passage is part of Jesus' Great Commission to his followers. Here Jesus gives us our mission in this world. Take time to understand what this passage says and means. Circle the repeated words. Underline the pronouns. Double underline the commands. Locate the important conjunctions (e.g., "therefore"). Identify the words or phrases that show means (i.e., how we do something), place, and time. Are there any lists? Do you see any promises? What is God's role? What is our role?

"make disciples"—This command lies at the heart of the Great Commission. A disciple is a committed follower of a teacher or leader (see Behaving 6). To "make" disciples involves (1) inviting people to begin a relationship with Jesus Christ and (2) helping them grow in that relationship. The command applies not just to the original hearers, but to all disciples. Otherwise his promise at the end of verse 20 would not make much sense.

"nations"—Although the word can refer to all nations except Israel, most scholars think the term refers to all peoples, including Israel. The full phrase "all nations" is used in Matthew 24:9, 14; 25:32 to refer to all peoples (cf. John 3:16). Matthew's gospel begins with Abraham (Matt. 1:1), through whom God promised to bless all peoples, and ends by showing that the promise will be fulfilled through Jesus and his missionary people.

"teaching them to obey"—Evangelism alone does not fulfill the Great Commission. New believers must enter a lifelong process of learning to obey Jesus' teachings. In Jesus' culture only privileged men had access to the leading rabbis. Jesus, however, invites **all** people to follow him. Teaching lies at the heart of the growth process, but this kind of teaching is much more than an academic exercise. Jesus does not say "teaching them to know," but rather "teaching them to obey." Discipleship is education that results in obedience (Matt. 12:49–50).

[18]Then Jesus came to them and said, "All authority in heaven

and on earth has been given to me. [19]Therefore go and make

disciples of all nations, baptizing them in the name of the

Father and of the Son and of the Holy Spirit, [20]and teaching

them to obey everything I have commanded you. And surely

I am with you always, to the very end of the age."

Fuel and Goal of Missions

Missions is not the ultimate goal of the church. Worship is. Missions exists because worship doesn't. Worship is ultimate, not missions, because God is ultimate, not man. When this age is over, and the countless millions of the redeemed fall on their faces before the throne of God, missions will be no more. It is a temporary necessity. But worship abides forever.

Worship, therefore, is the fuel and goal of missions. It's the goal of missions because in missions we simply aim to bring the nations into the white-hot enjoyment of God's glory. . . .

But worship is also the fuel of missions. Passion for God in worship precedes the offer of God in preaching. You can't commend what you don't cherish. . . .

Where passion for God is weak, zeal for missions will be weak.

—John Piper,
Let the Nations Be Glad, 17–18

The structure or organization of the Great Commission is very important. Look at each item below and the role that it plays in the commission. Then in the space after each item, answer the question, What difference does this make? In other words, what difference does it make that the foundation of the commands is the authority of Jesus? What difference does it make that "go" is as much a command as "make disciples"? And so forth.

- Foundation of the commands—"all authority . . . has been given to [Jesus]"

- Supporting command—"go"

- Main command—"make disciples of all nations"

- Explanation of how to carry out the commands (means)—"baptizing" and "teaching"

- Promise for those who carry out the commands—"I am with you always"

Crossing the Bridge

What theological principles do you see in Matthew 28:18–20?

-

-

-

So What?

1. What do you think Jesus' commission teaches us about how we should use terms such as *disciple* and *discipleship* today?

2. Does your Christian community put more emphasis on beginning the Christian faith (baptizing) or maturing in the faith (teaching)? If the emphasis is out of balance, how could it be adjusted?

3. What motivates you to be more involved in God's mission to rescue lost and hurting people? Try to be honest and specific.

4. What kind of teaching-learning are you experiencing on a weekly basis (e.g., sermons, Bible studies, small groups, personal study, books)?

5. What could make your teaching-learning experiences more focused on learning to obey rather than just learning to know?

6. The commission is to make disciples of all nations or peoples. What are you and your Christian community doing to reach out to people groups around your "world" and around the world?

Disciples = Christians

Everyone who has heard the gospel message and has responded by believing on Jesus for eternal life is a disciple/Christian/believer, all of which are virtually synonymous terms (cf. Acts 2:44; 4:32; 5:14; 6:1, 7; 11:26; 26:28).

Today many incorrectly use the title "disciple" to refer to a person who is more committed than other Christians or to those involved in special "discipleship programs." But we can see from Jesus' commission that all Christians are disciples. It is just that some are obedient disciples, while others are not.

—Michael Wilkins, *Matthew*, 956

Cross-References

Luke 24:45–49; John 17:18; 20:21–23; Acts 1:8; Rom. 10:14–15; 2 Cor. 5:11–20; 1 John 1:2–3

For Deeper Study

Piper, John. *Let the Nations Be Glad: The Supremacy of God in Missions*. 2nd ed. Rev. and exp. Grand Rapids: Baker, 2003.

Wilkins, Michael J. *Following the Master: A Biblical Theology of Discipleship*. Grand Rapids: Zondervan, 1992.

Wilkins, Michael J. *Matthew*. NIV Application Commentary. Grand Rapids: Zondervan, 2004.

Willard, Dallas. *The Great Omission: Reclaiming Jesus' Essential Teachings on Discipleship*. San Francisco: Harper Collins, 2006.

As the Father Has Sent Me, I Am Sending You

Engaging the World

God wants us to join him in his mission of rescuing people from the grip of Satan and sin. That's one reason why we are still on this earth. When Jesus appeared to his followers after his death and resurrection, he said, "Peace be with you! As the Father has sent me, I am sending you" (John 20:21). Our mission is clear—go and make disciples of all nations. But it will remain "mission impossible" unless we rely on the power of the Holy Spirit. God doesn't just give us a job to do and wish us good luck. The Holy Spirit empowers us to do the job of engaging the world with the good news of Jesus. Mark Tabb rightly concludes that "we cannot hide from our culture and change it at the same time" (*Mission to Oz*, 128). In Behaving 11 we will explore ways of living out our mission in this world.

Michael Green, senior research professor at Wycliffe Hall, Oxford University, has conducted a comprehensive study of how the early church lived out the Christian mission. At the beginning of his book titled *Evangelism in the Early Church*, he says that while it was the early church's conviction, passion, and determination that mattered most, they used at least five mission strategies, or methods, that could also prove useful for us (pages 23–27):

1. They did most of their evangelism on secular ground. Wherever they went, they talked about Jesus to anyone who would listen.
2. The early Christians made a priority of personal conversations with individuals. Jesus models this kind of face-to-face approach in his conversation with the woman at the well in John 4.

3. The home provided the most natural context for spreading the gospel. People gathered for food, companionship, learning, and worship in a non-threatening but intentional setting.

4. Church planting proved extremely effective. Green writes, "The leadership was always plural. . . . They were a leadership team. These new churches nearly always begin in a home, soon pack that out, and then hire a hall to meet in. Buildings come along later if at all" (page 25).

5. The first Christians emphasized the work of the Holy Spirit, who transformed their character and gifted them for ministry. Green concludes: "The Western Church has grown too dependent on words, and not nearly dependent enough on the power of the Holy Spirit. . . . Instead of being a community demonstrating the Lord's power, we have become one which talks incessantly" (v. 26). Yet the "kingdom of God is not a matter of talk but of power" (1 Cor. 4:20).

If you believe in engaging the world with the gospel of Jesus Christ but find yourself frustrated, guilt-ridden, or paralyzed when it comes to actually doing so, pray that God would use this teaching and your community group discussion to renew your perspective and passion for carrying out his mission in this world.

A Closer Look—Acts 1:7–8

In our focal passage, look for contrasts, time and place indicators, repeated pronouns, lists, cause-effect relationships, God's responsibility, and our responsibility.

⁷He said to them: "It is not for you to know the times or

dates the Father has set by his own authority. ⁸But you

will receive power when the Holy Spirit comes on you;

and you will be my witnesses in Jerusalem, and in all

Judea and Samaria, and to the ends of the earth."

THE POWER OF WORDS

"witnesses"—Those who receive the Spirit's power will be Jesus' witnesses. In Acts a witness is one who testifies to certain events and experiences. Read the verses in Acts listed below, and write beside each reference a brief description of what the witness actually testified about. You may have to read the surrounding context to get the full picture:

• 1:22

• 2:32

• 3:15

• 5:32

• 10:39

• 10:41

• 13:31

• 22:15

SCRIPTURE NOTES

Crossing the Bridge

How does our situation differ from that of the disciples who first heard Jesus speak these words?

What theological principles do you see in Acts 1:7–8?

-
-
-

A Comprehensive Strategy for Engaging the World

How can a Christian community today effectively engage the world with the good news of Jesus Christ? The strategy below is more than just another evangelistic program. Rather, it offers a comprehensive and realistic way of carrying out Jesus' mission in this world. We should always remember that apart from the empowering of God's Spirit, no plan will work.

1. We need to be attentive to how we *live the gospel* ourselves. People today are weary of words. They want to see a changed life before they will listen to any explanation of what caused the change. The integrity of the messenger authenticates the reality of the message.
2. We need to *know God's kingdom story* well enough to be able to converse about the whole story regardless of where our conversation begins. This calls for improving our biblical literacy and our theological understanding of the Christian message. (The kingdom story is summarized in the Believing column of the overview, pages 16–17).
3. We need to be *connected to a Christian community* that embodies the life and teachings of Jesus. Again, people today are moved to faith as they observe and connect with a community where the kingdom story is fleshed out for all to see. (Read the sidebar quote on page 173 about how the early church did this.)
4. We need to pray that God's Spirit would cultivate in us a *compassion for people*. We should be sensitive to many things in others' lives—change, pain, discontentment, frustration, openness, and so on.
5. We need to *spend time with people who do not have a relationship with Jesus*. This social connection is probably the number one challenge

for most Christians, many of whom simply don't spend any time with non-Christians.

6. We need to engage non-Christians in *honest, authentic conversations* about God and Christ. Many Christians who are equipped to spout off a three-minute, canned gospel presentation have very little aptitude for a more in-depth conversation that centers around the kingdom story. Perhaps the greatest deterrent to these kinds of conversations is fear; yet as Mark Tabb says, "If the gospel is true, it has nothing to fear from conversations with those who don't believe it" (*Mission to Oz*, 114). We must be equipped to listen effectively and to ask questions that will help us understand, not only people's life experiences, but also the story they are counting on to make sense of life.

7. We need to embody the kingdom story through genuinely spiritual responses (fruit of the Spirit in Galatians 5) and *authentic acts of service*. We should not serve for any payoff or personal profit but simply as an expression of God's love.

8. We need to *be the relational bridge* between our non-Christian friends and our Christian community. Today people will often make a commitment to a community where Jesus Christ can be experienced before they will make an individual commitment to Christ. Our relationship serves as the bridge between the church and the world.

9. We need to encourage our friends to make a *personal commitment to Jesus*. Simply being in the community is not enough. Conversion occurs when our friends decide to embrace God's kingdom story as their own so that they become part of the story line.

10. We need to journey with our friends in the *lifelong process* of allowing the Holy Spirit to conform us to the image of Jesus (see Behaving 7, pages 115–16).

So What?

1. When you study "witnessing" in Acts, you will see that the early Christians had a message with content—Jesus is the Messiah, he fulfilled the Scriptures, he was crucified and buried, he has been raised from the dead, and people need to repent and believe the good news. Their witnessing went far beyond a personal testimony of "what God was doing in their lives." In your view, how does witnessing today compare with the witnessing of the early church?

A Different People

Christians are distinguished from other men neither by country nor language nor the customs they observe. For they neither inhabit cities of their own, nor employ a peculiar form of speech, nor lead a life which is marked out by any singularity. . . . But inhabiting Greek as well as barbarian cities . . . and following the customs of the natives in respect of clothing, food, and the rest of their ordinary conduct, they display to us their wonderful and confessedly paradoxical manner of life. They dwell in fatherlands of their own country, but only as aliens. As citizens they share in all things with others, and yet endure all things as foreigners. . . . They marry as do all; they beget children, but they do not destroy their offspring. They have a common table, but not a common bed. They are in the flesh but they do not live after the flesh. They pass their days on earth, but they are citizens of heaven. They obey the prescribed laws, and at the same time surpass the laws by their lives. They love all men, and are persecuted by all.

—from the early second-century *Epistle to Diognetus*, quoted in Michael Green, *Evangelism in the Early Church*, 192

Cross-References
Mark 13:11; Luke 12:8–9; John 4:1–42;
17:15–19; Acts 4:18–20; 8:26–40; Rom.
1:16; 10:9–10; 1 Cor. 2:1–5; 9:19–27;
1 Thess. 1:5; 2 Tim. 1:7–8; 1 Peter 3:15

For Deeper Study
Green, Michael. *Evangelism in the Early Church.*
Rev. ed. Grand Rapids: Eerdmans, 2003.
Kallenberg, Brad. *Live to Tell: Evangelism to a
Postmodern Age.* Grand Rapids: Brazos
Press, 2002.
Long, Jimmy. *Emerging Hope: Strategy for
Reaching Postmodern Generations.* 2nd
ed. Downers Grove, IL: InterVarsity Press,
2004.
Newman, Randy. *Questioning Evangelism:
Engaging People's Hearts the Way Jesus
Did.* Grand Rapids: Kregel, 2004.
Tabb, Mark. *Mission to Oz: Reaching Postmod-
erns Without Losing Your Way.* Chicago:
Moody, 2004.

2. Some would say that we spend too much time talking about strategies and methods when we should be focusing on imitating the conviction, passion, and determination of the early church. How would
you respond to that sentiment?

3. As you look at the ten-step engagement strategy outlined in Behaving 11, what are your two strongest areas? In what two areas do you
want to grow?

4. Michael Green suggests that one of the great needs of the church
today is for "those who evangelize to improve their theological
understanding, and for those who are theologically competent to
come out of their ivory tower and evangelize" (*Evangelism in the Early
Church*, 19). What are your ideas for achieving this integration of
head, heart, and hands?

5. What is one thing your Christian community could do differently to
become more faithful in living out the Great Commission?

Who Cares?

Compassion

Our mission is to go and make disciples of all nations. To fulfill this mission we must get out of our comfortable "Christian" cocoons and subcultures and touch a world full of people looking for life apart from God. As we engage non-Christians in open, honest conversations, we start to see their deep need for a relationship with the one true source of life, Jesus Christ. When we hear their stories, we see them less as a target for soul-winning and more as a person created in God's image who needs to experience life and hope. Instead of condemning or avoiding or manipulating, we begin to feel compassion and sympathy. Our hearts go out to them, and we are led by the Spirit to give our time, possessions, and abilities to draw our friends into a relationship with our Lord. In Becoming 11 we will see that a heart of compassion is more valuable than pious credentials or legalistic purity.

Notice how Jesus' compassion caused him to heal, feed, touch, cleanse, teach, exorcise demons, raise the dead, and forgive the rebellious. The italicized words in these verses all represent the same Greek word:

When Jesus . . . saw a large crowd, he had *compassion* on them and healed their sick. (Matt. 14:14)

Jesus . . . said, "I have *compassion* for these people; they have already been with me three days and have nothing to eat. I do not want to send them away hungry, or they may collapse on the way." (Matt. 15:32)

Jesus had *compassion* on them [two blind men] and touched their eyes. Immediately they received their sight and followed him. (Matt. 20:34)

Filled with *compassion*, Jesus reached out his hand and touched the man. "I am willing," he said. "Be clean!" Immediately the leprosy left him and he was cured. (Mark 1:41–42).

"You have answered correctly . . . Do this and you will live"—In Luke 10:28 Jesus tells the expert in religious law that he had answered the question correctly or accurately (*orthōs*, from which we get our word *orthodox*). But Jesus doesn't stop with "That's the right answer." He adds, "Do this and you will live." Then Jesus tells the parable with its surprise ending—a Samaritan rather than a Jew acts as the neighbor (the hero). Jesus again tells the expert in religious law to "go and do likewise" (cf. the original question in 10:25). Compassion means more than giving the right answer in a theological discussion; it is love demonstrated in sacrificial action.

"took pity"—Here we have a window into the Samaritan's heart. This word "pity" speaks of mercy, sympathy, or tenderhearted compassion. The same word is used in the parable of the prodigal son, where the Father has compassion on his rebellious son (see Luke 15:20). Showing pity, or compassion, causes us to give our time, possessions, abilities, and influence to help a person in need. Instead of "passing by" because of fear or pride, the Samaritan uses his own clothes, oil, wine, donkey, money, and time to take care of the Jewish victim. That's compassion!

When Jesus landed and saw a large crowd, he had *compassion* on them, because they were like sheep without a shepherd. So he began teaching them many things. (Mark 6:34)

It has often thrown him [a demon-possessed boy] into fire or water to kill him. But if you can do anything, *take pity* on us and help us. (Mark 9:22)

When the Lord saw her [a grieving widow], his *heart went out* to her and he said, "Don't cry." (Luke 7:13)

But while he was still a long way off, his father saw him and was filled with *compassion* for him; he ran to his son. (Luke 15:20)

John Stott helps us see what was going on with Jesus:

The eyes of Jesus never missed the sight of need. Nobody could accuse him of being like the priest and the Levite [in the parable of the good Samaritan]. . . . Of both it is written, "he saw him." Yet each saw him without seeing, for he looked the other way, and so "passed by on the other side." Jesus, on the other hand, truly "saw." He was not afraid to look human need in the face, in all its ugly reality. And what he saw invariably moved him to compassion, and so to . . . service. . . . He saw, he felt, he acted. The movement was from the eye to the heart, and from the heart to the hand. His compassion was always aroused by the sight of need, and it always led to constructive action. (*Authentic Christianity*, 37)

A Closer Look—Luke 10:30–37

Find Luke 10 in your Bible. Read about Jesus' encounter with an expert in religious law in 10:25–29. Jesus answers this man's question with a parable—a story that teaches at least one spiritual lesson. Jesus' story is known as the parable of the good Samaritan.

1. Read Luke 10:30–37 carefully and answer the story questions below.

WHO?	WHAT?

WHEN?	WHERE?
WHY?	**HOW?**

2. Consult a Bible handbook, dictionary, or background commentary to find out more about the following elements of the story. Make a few notes summarizing what you have found.

- Jerusalem to Jericho

- A priest and a Levite

- A Samaritan

Why do you think the expert in religious law said "the one" in verse 37 rather than "the Samaritan"?

Create a scenario that we might experience today that illustrates the same truths as Jesus' parable. Don't worry about writing a full-blown story; just think of a parallel situation.

Crossing the Bridge

What biblical principles do you see in Luke 10:30–37?

-

-

-

-

So What?

1. How has God spoken to you through the parable of the good Samaritan?

2. What kinds of things cause us to "pass by on the other side"?

3. What motivates you to show compassion?

4. Read "Role Reversal" in the sidebar and create your own scenario to illustrate what compassion might look like in our contemporary setting.

5. How do you think God wants us to relate sharing the good news of Jesus Christ (evangelism) with meeting people's physical and social needs (social ministry)? How would you rate your own grasp of this important relationship?

6. As a result of this section on mission, engaging the world, and compassion, what small steps does God want you to take to carry out his mission in this world? How can you help others with the task?

Cross-References

1 Sam. 15:22; Isa. 58:6–7; Mic. 6:8; Matt. 9:9–13; Eph. 4:32; James 2:14–26; 1 Peter 3:8; 1 John 3:17–18

For Deeper Study

Blomberg, Craig L. *Interpreting the Parables.* Downers Grove, IL: InterVarsity Press, 1990.

Bock, Darrell. *Luke.* NIV Application Commentary. Grand Rapids: Zondervan, 1996.

Sider, Ronald J. *Good News and Good Works.* Grand Rapids: Baker, 1993.

Wenham, David. *The Parables of Jesus.* Downers Grove, IL: InterVarsity Press, 1989.

The Grand Finale

The End

The kingdom story began with God creating humans to experience life and enjoy his presence forever. Although Satan and sin did a lot of damage in their bid to destroy the whole project, God's love would not let us go. He sent Jesus Christ to rescue us from the powers of darkness and restore our relationship with him. When we enter into this new relationship, we also become members of God's new community, the church. The Holy Spirit takes up residence within us and begins the process of making us more like Jesus Christ. To fully understand the kingdom story, we need to know how it ends, and that is the subject of Believing 12. (The technical term for the study of final or last things is *eschatology*.)

The story's final chapter is closely tied to Jesus' teaching about the kingdom of God. The kingdom of God is the rule or reign of God. When Jesus began to minister publicly, his main message was "The kingdom of God is near. Repent and believe the good news!" (Mark 1:15; see also Matt. 4:17, 23; Luke 4:42–44). Jesus healed the sick, cast out demons, fed the hungry, and forgave sinners—all signs that the kingdom had arrived. In Jesus, the kingdom of God became a *present reality* (Matt. 11:11–12; 12:28; 18:1–5; Luke 17:20–21). Because his first followers expected him to establish the kingdom fully and totally during their lifetimes, they were crushed when Jesus was crucified. Yet after his resurrection and ascension to heaven, the disciples began to see God's greater plan (see the chart below).

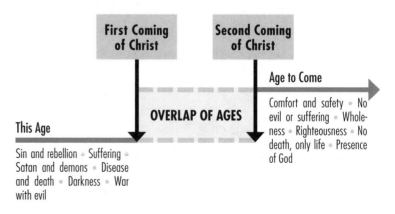

At Jesus' first coming, the kingdom of God broke into this world. A world filled with sin, rebellion, Satan, darkness, and evil encountered a touch of peace, righteousness, life, and God. When we begin to follow Christ the King, we start to experience "age-to-come" (eternal) life right now. We come alive and get a taste of heaven while still living on earth. The apostle Paul says that we have been "rescued . . . from the dominion of darkness and brought . . . into the kingdom of the Son" (Col. 1:13). We are new people living in an old world. God has started his kingdom project, but he has not completely finished it. The kingdom of God has *already* arrived, but it has *not yet* come in all its fullness. The grand project has been launched, but it has not been finished. The kingdom of God also has a *future dimension* (Matt. 6:10; 25:34; 26:29; Luke 19:11–27). We are living in enemy-occupied territory between God's initial invasion (Jesus' first coming) and his total defeat of evil (Jesus' second coming). We are living in the overlap between this age and the age to come. Our circumstance explains a lot.

- We experience God's forgiveness, but we still sin and will never be perfect in this life.
- We have victory over death, but we will one day die physically.
- We still get sick, and not all Christians will experience healing.
- We live in the Spirit, but Satan will continue to attack and may do damage.
- God lives within us, but we do not yet live in God's presence.

Because of the "already/not fully" reality of the kingdom of God, we will experience victories as well as struggles until Jesus returns—an event that Christians throughout history have longed for. The return of Christ lies at the heart of our focal passage from 1 Thessalonians.

A Closer Look—1 Thessalonians 4:13–18

In this section of his letter, Paul is responding to his readers' confusion about the return of Christ and the events associated with it, especially the resurrection from the dead. In the blank space to the right of the passage, *outline Paul's train of thought* as he seeks to give these believers hope by answering their questions.

SCRIPTURE NOTES

¹³Brothers and sisters, we do not want you to be uninformed

about those who sleep in death, so that you do not grieve

like the rest, who have no hope. ¹⁴We believe that Jesus died

and rose again, and so we believe that God will bring with

Jesus those who have fallen asleep in him. [15]According to the Lord's word, we tell you that we who are still alive, who are left till the coming of the Lord, will certainly not precede those who have fallen asleep. [16]For the Lord himself will come down from heaven, with a loud command, with the voice of the archangel and with the trumpet call of God, and the dead in Christ will rise first. [17]After that, we who are still alive and are left will be caught up together with them in the clouds to meet the Lord in the air. And so we will be with the Lord forever. [18]Therefore encourage one another with these words. (TNIV)

Crossing the Bridge

What theological principles do you see in 1 Thessalonians 4:13–18?

-
-
-

Important Parts in the Story's Last Chapter

The end of God's kingdom story includes many important topics. Here are the main ones.

Death

One thing is certain in life—we will all die (Rom. 5:12; 6:23). The time of our death is beyond our control (Eccl. 8:8; James 4:14). Although death is described as the last enemy (1 Cor. 15:26), Christ has conquered death, and those who follow Christ don't have to fear death (Ps. 23:4; Phil. 1:21). When Christ returns, he will kill death (1 Cor. 15:54–56).

The Second Coming of Jesus

Whereas his first coming was humble, Jesus' second coming will be a public, visible, spectacular event (Matt. 24:30–31; Heb. 9:28). His coming will

---

When the Play Ends

Why is God landing in this enemy-occupied world in disguise and starting a sort of secret society to undermine the devil? Why is He not landing in force, invading it? Is it that He is not strong enough? Well, Christians think He is going to land in force; we do not know when. But we can guess why He is delaying. He wants to give us the chance of joining His side freely. I do not suppose you and I would have thought much of a Frenchman who waited till the Allies were marching into Germany and then announced he was on our side. God will invade. But I wonder whether people who ask God to interfere so openly and directly in our

(continued on the next page)

BELIEVING 12—*The End*

be sudden—like a thief in the night (Matt. 24:44; 1 Thess. 5:1–3)—and only the Father knows the time (Matt. 24:36). Jesus will return to gather his people, judge the wicked, and establish his kingdom in all its fullness (Matt. 25:31–32; Rev. 19:11–16).

The Resurrection of the Dead

All people will be raised from the dead (John 5:23–29). Believers will be raised to eternal life (John 6:40), while unbelievers will be raised in order to be condemned (Matt. 25:46; John 5:29). Christians will be given resurrection bodies (1 Cor. 15), created for perfect life in the new heaven and new earth.

The Last Judgment

All people will face judgment after death (2 Tim. 4:1; Heb. 9:27). Christians will not be condemned for their sin (John 5:24; Rom. 8:1–2), but we must give an account for how we lived our lives (Rom. 14:12; 1 Cor. 3:12–15; 2 Cor. 5:10). Our Judge will also be our Savior (John 5:22; Acts 10:42). Unbelievers will be condemned because they have not trusted in Christ (John 12:48; 2 Peter 3:7; Jude 15; Rev. 20:15).

Hell or Heaven

Hell is a real place of punishment for those who reject Jesus (Matt. 13:39–43; 25:41; Rev. 20:15). People in hell experience the darkness of eternal separation from God (Matt. 25:46; 2 Thess. 1:9). In contrast, heaven is the eternal home of God's people. In the new heaven and new earth, we will live an embodied life (1 Cor. 15:35–37), a community life (Rev. 21:1–3), a pain-free, sin-free, death-free life (Rev. 21:4), a worshipful life (Rev. 21:22), a life of meaningful work (Rev. 22:3, 5), a diverse life (Rev. 22:2), and a God-centered life (Rev. 22:4). What God originally planned for the garden of Eden will finally come to pass in the heavenly garden, all because of the battle won in the garden of Gethsemane.

So What?

1. Some of us are "already" Christians (naive optimists who expect perfection now), while others are "not fully" Christians (gloomy pessimists overwhelmed by human problems). Which one are you most like? How can you become more of an "already/not fully" Christian, a biblical realist who admits struggles *and* celebrates victories?

world quite realise what it will be like when He does. When that happens, it is the end of the world. When the author walks on to the stage the play is over. God is going to invade, all right: but what is the good of saying you are on His side then, when you see the whole natural universe melting away like a dream and something else—something it never entered your head to conceive—comes crashing in; something so beautiful to some of us and so terrible to others that none of us will have any choice left? For this time it will be God without disguise; something so overwhelming that it will strike either irresistible love or irresistible horror into every creature. It will be too late then to choose your side. There is no use saying you choose to lie down when it has become impossible to stand up. That will not be the time for choosing: it will be the time when we discover which side we really have chosen, whether we realised it before or not. Now, today, this moment is our chance to choose the right side. God is holding back to give us that chance. It will not last forever. We must take it or leave it.

—C. S. Lewis,
Mere Christianity, 64–65

Cross-References

Matt. 24–25; Mark 13; 1 Cor. 15:12–58; 1 Thess. 5:1–11; 2 Peter 3:3–14; Rev. 19–22

For Deeper Study

Beale, G. K. *1–2 Thessalonians*. IVP New Testament Commentary. Downers Grove, IL: InterVarsity Press, 2003.

Hays, J. Daniel, J. Scott Duvall, and C. Marvin Pate. *Dictionary of Biblical Prophecy and End Times*. Grand Rapids: Zondervan, 2007.

Holmes, Michael W. *1 and 2 Thessalonians*. NIV Application Commentary. Grand Rapids: Zondervan, 1998.

2. Think about the theological principles you listed under "Crossing the Bridge." What is the main message you see in 1 Thessalonians 4:13–18?

3. Do you think all the talk about things like the tribulation, the rapture, the Antichrist, Armageddon, and the millennium prevents us from seeing the main message about how the story ends? Explain your thinking.

4. Does the ending of God's kingdom story surprise you in any way? Would you have planned things differently? Why?

5. Do you think knowing more about how the story ends will affect your life in any way right now?

6. In light of how the story ends, what should be the focus of our Christian community?

The Wilderness

Persevering

The Bible closes with Jesus' words, "I am coming soon," followed by the response, "Come, Lord Jesus." (Rev. 22:20). The next line, the very last line in the entire Bible, reads, "The grace of the Lord Jesus be with God's people. Amen" (v. 21). That makes sense. Christians who are dealing with tough times actually long for Christ's return. His coming will mean an end to pain, sickness, injustice, sin, Satan, and death. But while we await his return, we need grace to remain faithful and stay the course. As John Ortberg reminds us, "God takes his people to the Promised Land by way of the desert. He is the God of the roundabout way" (*Love Beyond Reason*, 83). The wilderness is not a fun place, but it can be a formative place as we learn to trust God at a deeper level. Behaving 12 is about the need to obey God, not only when we feel his presence, but also when he seems silent and distant. We are called to endure a long-distance race, not a sprint.

W hen I was in college, I ran the Dallas White Rock marathon. In case you're not into running, a marathon is a little over twenty-six miles. My friend Kenny Burt and I trained for four months. Sometimes those late afternoon runs of six, eight, or twelve miles were fun, and we felt like we could run forever. At other times, even a four-mile run would drain us and leave us discouraged and doubting. Neither of us had ever run twenty-six miles, and we weren't sure if we could actually do it. But we kept training, whether we felt like it or not. Day after day, we pounded the pavement. We endured heat, rude drivers, leg cramps, wind, cold, darkness, rain, exhaustion, and thirst in order to run the Rock in December. The big day arrived and, loaded with carbohydrates, we began the race. I've never felt a surge of adrenaline like I felt during those first few miles. We settled into a pace for the next ten to fifteen miles. Then around mile eighteen or so, we entered "cloud of witnesses"—The great "cloud" refers to the heroes of faith mentioned in Hebrews 11. How are they witnesses? While it's possible that they are spectators watching our every move, it's more likely that they bear witness to God's faithfulness. They persevered and found God faithful. Rather than the heroes watching us, we are looking to them for encouragement that perseverance is worth the price.

"everything that hinders"—This refers to a weight, burden, or hindrance. In the ancient world runners would shed any excess weight in order to move freely and run faster (some ran naked). Sin certainly entangles us, as the next part of the sentence makes clear, but some things that are not sinful in themselves may weigh us down. We should get rid of anything that hinders our passionate devotion to Christ.

"run with perseverance"—This figure of speech reminds us that the Christian life requires action and effort. God expects us to "run." Also, the race we run is more like a marathon and less like a short sprint. To run with perseverance means to persist and stick with it over a lifetime, through easy times as well as hard times.

"race marked out"—This phrase means to "lie before." As runners see the course marked out before them, so Christians see the path of endurance laid out for us. We see where we must go, but actually running the race is the hard part.

new territory. We got separated and were running alone. I experienced severe leg cramps. The wind was very strong that day, and, like it or not, I had to stop and stretch many times. Both of us hit "the wall"—a common experience for marathoners around mile twenty, where your body completely runs out of gas. I kept on putting one foot in front of the other, not knowing for sure if mile twenty-six would ever arrive. Through pain, strong winds, utter fatigue, and a constant urge to quit, I persevered to the end. We both finished the race. We never talked much about who "won" since we both came to understand winning as just finishing the grueling twenty-six-mile race. It was an unforgettable experience.

The Bible speaks of life as an endurance race in Hebrews 12:1–2. Take a moment and read Hebrews 11. What is your first reaction to those who endured the race of faith?

Perseverance is a prominent theme in the New Testament. Below you will find a few key places where perseverance is mentioned (the actual translation is given in parentheses). Read each passage and its surrounding context, and write a short statement in the space provided, explaining how perseverance is significant in this setting.

- Matthew 24:13 ("stands firm")

- Luke 8:15 ("persevering")

- Romans 2:7 ("persistence")

- Romans 5:3–4 ("perseverance")

- 2 Corinthians 1:6 ("patient endurance")

- Colossians 1:10–12 ("endurance")

- 1 Thessalonians 1:3 ("endurance")

- 2 Thessalonians 1:4 ("perseverance")

- 2 Thessalonians 3:5 ("perseverance")

- Hebrews 10:36 ("persevere")

- James 1:2–4 ("perseverance")

- James 1:12 ("perseveres")

- James 5:11 ("persevered")

A Closer Look—Hebrews 12:1–2

As you look closely at our focal passage, notice conjunctions, reasons, figures of speech, commands, descriptions, lists, contrasts, important words, and so on. Also note that this text has one main command (in bold) surrounded by three supporting statements.

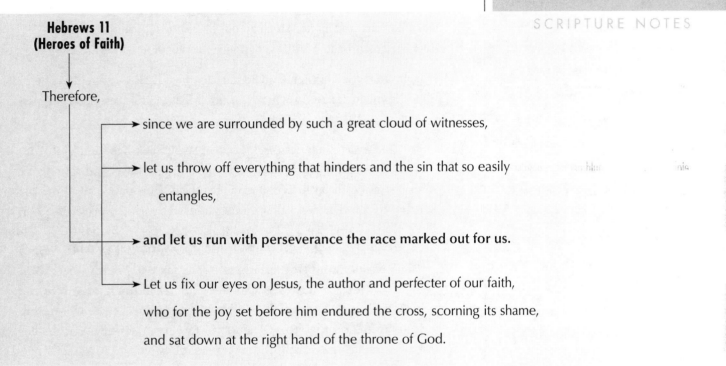

**Hebrews 11
(Heroes of Faith)**

Therefore,

since we are surrounded by such a great cloud of witnesses,

let us throw off everything that hinders and the sin that so easily

entangles,

and let us run with perseverance the race marked out for us.

Let us fix our eyes on Jesus, the author and perfecter of our faith,

who for the joy set before him endured the cross, scorning its shame,

and sat down at the right hand of the throne of God.

Crossing the Bridge

What theological principles do you see in Hebrews 12:1–2?

-

-

-

At some point every Christian walks through the wilderness. John of the Cross, who endured persecution and imprisonment for his faith, referred to this spiritual desert as the "dark night of the soul"—a time when we don't feel God's presence, when God doesn't seem to answer prayer or speak

BEHAVING 12—*Persevering*

187

through his Word, when worship is dull and temptation grows stronger. We lack passion and direction, and God seems far away. In a word, we feel forsaken. We confess our sin, we plead with God for guidance, and nothing seems to bring back the good old days of sweet communion with our Lord. Richard Foster refers to this experience as "God's purifying silence."

> Through all of this, paradoxically, God is purifying our faith by threatening to destroy it. We are led to a profound and holy distrust of all superficial drives and human strivings. We know more deeply than ever before our capacity for infinite self-deception. Slowly we are being taken off of vain securities and false allegiances. Our trust in all exterior and interior results is being shattered so that we can learn faith in God alone. Through our barrenness of soul God is producing detachment, humility, patience, perseverance. (*Prayer*, 22)

In a chapter titled "When God Seems Distant," Rick Warren offers helpful advice about what to do when you don't feel God's presence (*Purpose-Driven Life*, 110–13):

1. *Tell God exactly how you feel.* Pour out your heart to God (Job 7:11; 29:4). Unloading your feelings on God through prayer can actually be a confession of faith (see "Prayer Paralysis?" on page 159). Pray the lament Psalms as ways of speaking honestly with God (see Pss. 3–8, 10, 12–13, 15–17, 21–22, 25–26, 28, 31, 35, 38, 42–44, 51, 54–61, 69–71, 74, 79–80, 83, 86, 88, 90, 94, 102, 109, 120, 130–132, 139–141, 143).
2. *Think back to what God has already done for you.* You can trust God for the future because you can trace his faithfulness to you in the past. Reflect on how much God has already done for you by sending Jesus to die on the cross. Then turn to your own life and consider how God has been faithful to you personally.
3. *Focus on God's unchanging character.* God's nature does not change even when our circumstances do. Remind yourself that God is good and loving, great and powerful, that he has a plan for your life and that he is in control.
4. *Trust God to keep his promises.* God's word is more reliable than our emotions. Trust that God is doing a work in your life although you simply don't understand it at the moment.

So What?

1. Right now in your life, what does it involve for you to persevere or endure?

2. In our focal passage there is one main command surrounded by three supporting statements. If we neglect these supports, it will be more difficult to carry out the main command to run with perseverance. Evaluate how you are doing in the supporting areas.

  a. How can you find encouragement from those who have already persevered? Do you read the Scriptures consistently? Do you read biographies of influential Christians of the past?

  b. Sin certainly causes us to stumble, but are there also permissible things in your life that might not be profitable? What is hindering your ability to persevere?

  c. How Jesus-focused are you? It's easy to focus on good things, even religious things, and lose focus on Jesus Christ. When is the last time you read the Gospels?

3. Have you ever been through a "dark night" or "trough"? How did God change you through this experience? What dangers to our faith does the dark night bring?

4. What role should our feelings play in our relationship with God?

5. In addition to the advice given by Rick Warren earlier, what helps you to persevere in the wilderness?

than during the peak periods, that it is growing into the sort of creature He wants it to be. Hence the prayers offered in the state of dryness are those which please Him best. . . . He cannot "tempt" to virtue as we do to vice. He wants them to learn to walk and must therefore take away His hand; and if only the will to walk is there He is pleased even with their stumbles. . . . Our [Satan's] cause is never more in danger than when a human, no longer desiring, but still intending, to do our Enemy's [God's] will, looks round upon a universe from which every trace of Him seems to have vanished, and asks why he has been forsaken, and still obeys.

—C. S. Lewis,
Screwtape Letters, 38–40

Cross-References
See the Scripture references on pages 186–87 with regard to perseverance.

For Deeper Study
Carson, D. A. *How Long, O, Lord? Reflections on Suffering and Evil*. Grand Rapids: Baker, 1990.

Guthrie, George H. *Hebrews*. NIV Application Commentary. Grand Rapids: Zondervan, 1998.

Lewis, C. S. *The Problem of Pain*. New York: Macmillan, 1962.

Yancey, Philip. *Reaching for the Invisible God*. Grand Rapids: Zondervan, 2000.

Yancey, Philip. *Where Is God When It Hurts?* Anniversary edition. Grand Rapids: Zondervan, 2002.

Are We There Yet?

Hope

Do you ever feel like a kid riding in the back seat of a car, asking God that old, familiar question, "Are we there yet?" or "How much farther?" That is actually a very biblical question, asked by many faithful followers (cf. Pss. 6:3; 13:1; 35:17; 89:46; Hab. 1:2; Rev. 6:10). The good news is that the story does have an ending. The bad news is that we aren't there yet. As Craig Barnes says, "Christians will always live carrying in one hand the promises of how it will be and in the other hand the reality of how it is" (*Yearning*, 16). God is taking us somewhere. There is a real destination, but we haven't arrived. We're still on the journey. As a result, we are called to persevere. In order to survive this time between the "already" and the "not fully," we need hope; Becoming 12 is about biblical hope.

In our culture, the word *hope* is almost as confusing as the word *love*. We can say "I hope it doesn't rain at our reception," or "I hope the Dallas Cowboys make the playoffs," or "I put my hope in Christ." To understand what the Bible means by hope, we first need to know what it does not mean. In the Bible hope is not the same thing as wishing for something, as in wishing against rain or for the Cowboys. When you wish for something, you have no assurance that it will happen and no basis for "hoping" one way or the other. Our wishes have no connection to reality.

Unlike wishful thinking, biblical hope is *based on the character of God*. Nothing is more sure and certain. We know God's character because of what he has done in the past and what he is doing in the present. In the past, God defeated sin and Satan through the death and resurrection of his Son, Jesus Christ. In the present God has given us his very own Spirit, who is his "seal" of ownership and protection as well as a "deposit guaranteeing" our future inheritance (Eph. 1:13–14). Our hope is more than wishing, because our hope rests on God's character. God himself is our hope. Our future is certain.

Biblical hope is a confident reliance on God to stay true to his word and keep his promises. Hope is a disciplined (1 Peter 1:13), sacrificial (1 Cor. 9:24–27), purifying (1 John 3:3), joyful (Rom. 12:12) waiting on the Lord. As the old song says, "This world is not my home. I'm just passing through." We are journeying to a more permanent home, a heavenly home (Heb. 11:10, 16). Hope means living in the present in light of a rock-solid certain future. This future is based on the character of God, and we know who God is because of what he has done and is doing. We will "get there" because our Father always keeps his promises.

Our focal passage is Romans 8:22–25, a text that tells the true story of our present struggles and our hope for the future. Enjoy!

A Closer Look—Romans 8:22–25

Read the focal passage carefully, looking at prepositional phrases, repeated words, time indicators, explanations, purpose statements, contrasts, figures of speech, and so on.

²²We know that the whole creation has been groaning as in the pains of childbirth right up to the present time. ²³Not only so, but we ourselves, who have the firstfruits of the Spirit, groan inwardly as we wait eagerly for our adoption as sons, the redemption of our bodies. ²⁴For in this hope we were saved. But hope that is seen is no hope at all. Who hopes for what he already has? ²⁵But if we hope for what we do not yet have, we wait for it patiently.

1. From the context, why does creation and why do Christians "groan"?

Hopelessness Is Hell

Living without hope is no longer living. Hell is hopelessness and it is not for nothing that at the entrance to Dante's hell there stand the words: "Abandon hope, all you who enter here."

—Jürgen Moltmann,
Theology of Hope, 32

"firstfruits of the Spirit"—The Holy Spirit serves as God's promise that he is not finished with us yet. The Spirit is like a down payment or a pledge guaranteeing our future. The Spirit is the unbreakable connection between the beginning and the end of our experience of God's salvation (cf. 2 Cor. 1:22; 5:5; Eph. 1:14). The Spirit joins the "already" to the "not fully" in God's great salvation story.

"redemption of our bodies"—In Romans 8:14–17 we read that Christians have already been adopted as God's children. A few verses later we read that "we wait eagerly for our adoption" (v. 23). So have we already been adopted or not? Yes, when we entered a relationship with Jesus, we were adopted as God's children, but there is more to our adoption—the redemption of [not from] our bodies. What we experience now is real, but there is more to come. Redemption is both past and future. We are God's children now, but one day God will transform our bodies into bodies fit for a new heaven and new earth (see 1 Cor. 15).

"wait for it patiently"—Between the already and the not fully, we hope and wait. The word "patiently" could be translated "with endurance" or "with perseverance." This is the same word that we encountered in Hebrews 12:1–2 (see Behaving 12). We persevere through hardship and suffering, waiting for Christ to return.

2. List all the characteristics of hope you can find in this passage.

Crossing the Bridge

What biblical principles do you see in Romans 8:22–25?

-
-
-

The Beginning and the End

"In the beginning God . . ." so the story begins. We were created to experience perfect community, but Satan and sin entered the picture and brought death. Because of his love, God came to our rescue. Through the life, death, and resurrection of Jesus, the gift of his Holy Spirit, and his new community the church, God is reversing the curse (see chart, pages 192–93). He wants us to experience life and hope. That is his heart, and our opportunity. To God be the glory!

GENESIS 1–11	REVELATION 19–22	
Sinful people scattered	God's people unite to sing his praises	19:6–7
"Marriage" of Adam and Eve	Marriage of Last Adam and his bride, the church	19:7; 21:2, 9
God abandoned by sinful people	God's people (New Jerusalem, bride of Christ) made ready for God; marriage of Lamb	19:7–8; 21:2, 9–21
Exclusion from bounty of Eden	Invitation to marriage supper of Lamb	19:9
Satan introduces sin into world	Satan and sin are judged	19:11–21; 20:7–10
The Serpent deceives humanity	The ancient Serpent is bound "to keep him from deceiving the nations"	20:2–3
God gives humans dominion over the earth	God's people will reign with him forever	20:4, 6; 22:5
People rebel against the true God resulting in physical and spiritual death	God's people risk death to worship the true God and thus experience life	20:4–6
Sinful people sent away from life	God's people have their names written in the Book of Life	20:4–6, 15; 21:6, 27

Death enters the world	Death is put to death	20:14; 21:4
God creates first heaven and earth, eventually cursed by sin	God creates a new heaven and earth where sin is nowhere to be found	21:1
Water symbolizes unordered chaos	There is no longer any sea (symbol of evil)	21:1
Sin brings pain and tears	God comforts his people and removes crying and pain	21:4
Sinful humanity cursed with wandering (exile)	God's people given a permanent home	21:3
Community forfeited	Genuine community experienced	21:3, 7
Sinful people are banished from presence of God	God lives among his people	21:3, 7, 22; 22:4
Creation begins to grow old and die	All things are made new	21:5
Water used to destroy wicked humanity	God quenches thirst with water from spring of life	21:6; 22:1
"In the beginning God . . ."	"I am the Alpha and the Omega, the Beginning and the End."	21:6
Sinful humanity suffers a wandering exile in the land	God gives his children an inheritance	21:7
Sin enters the world	Sin banished from God's city	21:8, 27; 22:15
Sinful humanity separated from presence of holy God	God's people experience God's holiness (cubed city = Holy of Holies)	21:15–21
God creates light and separates it from darkness	No more night or natural light; God himself is the source of light	21:23; 22:5
Languages of sinful humanity confused	God's people is a multicultural people	21:24, 26; 22:2
Sinful people sent away from garden	New heaven/earth includes a garden	22:2
Sinful people forbidden to eat from tree of life	God's people may eat freely from the tree of life	22:2, 14
Sin results in spiritual sickness	God heals the nations	22:2
Sinful people cursed	The curse removed from redeemed humanity and they become a blessing	22:3
Sinful people refuse to serve/obey God	God's people serve him	22:3
Sinful people ashamed in God's presence	God's people will "see his face"	22:4

Chart taken from *The Story of Israel* by J. Daniel Hays, C. Marvin Pate, E. Randolph Richards, W. Dennis Tucker Jr., Preben Vang, and J. Scott Duvall. Copyright © 2004 by J. Daniel Hays, C. Marvin Pate, E. Randolph Richards, W. Dennis Tucker Jr., Preben Vang, and J. Scott Duvall. Used with permission of InterVarsity Press, PO Box 1400, Downers Grove, IL 60515. http://www.ivpress.com/.

Not Just a New Heaven

Then I saw a new heaven and a new earth, for the old heaven and the old earth had disappeared. And the sea was also gone. And I saw the holy city, the new Jerusalem, coming down from God out of heaven like a beautiful bride prepared for her husband. I heard a loud shout from the throne, saying, "Look, the home of God is now among his people! He will live with them, and they will be his people. God himself will be with them. He will remove all of their sorrows, and there will be no more death or sorrow or crying or pain. For the old world and its evils are gone forever." And the one sitting on the throne said, "Look, I am making all things new!" And then he said to me, "Write this down, for what I tell you is trustworthy and true." And he also said, "It is finished! I am the Alpha and the Omega—the Beginning and the End. To all who are thirsty I will give the springs of the water of life without charge! All who are victorious will inherit all these blessings, and I will be their God, and they will be my children.

—Revelation 21:1–7 NLT

Cross-References

Pss. 33:18; 42:5; 62:5; 130:5; Isa. 40:31; 65:17–21; Rom. 5:1–5; 12:12; 15:4, 13; 1 Cor. 15; Eph. 1:18–19; Col. 1:27; 1 Thess. 1:3; 2 Tim. 4:8; Titus 2:13; 3:4–7; Heb. 10:23; 1 Peter 1:3–9, 13; 3:15; 1 John 3:2–3

For Deeper Study

Dockery, David S. *Our Christian Hope.* Nashville: LifeWay, 1998.

Long, Jimmy. *Emerging Hope: Strategy for Reaching Postmodern Generations.* 2nd ed. Downers Grove, IL: InterVarsity Press, 2004.

Moo, Douglas J. *Romans.* NIV Application Commentary. Grand Rapids: Zondervan, 2000.

So What?

1. What is the difference between wishful thinking and biblical hope?

2. What most excites you about our permanent home?

3. Is the biblical concept of a resurrected body in the new heaven and new earth different from the concept of heaven you have heard about all your life?

4. As you read through the Genesis-Revelation chart above, which lines stand out the most to you? Why?

5. What can you and your community do to help you experience hope at a deeper level?

6. How can your Christian community better communicate hope to a culture that is desperate for hope?

~ The End ~

and the beginning

Barnes, M. Craig. *Yearning: Living Between How It Is and How It Ought to Be*. Downers Grove, IL: InterVarsity Press, 1992.

Blomberg, Craig L. *1 Corinthians*. NIV Application Commentary. Grand Rapids: Zondervan, 1995.

———. *Matthew*. New American Commentary. Nashville: Broadman & Holman, 1992.

Bonhoeffer, Dietrich. *The Cost of Discipleship*. New York: Macmillan, 1963.

———. *Life Together*. San Francisco: HarperSanFrancisco, 1954.

Boyd, Gregory A. *Repenting of Religion: Turning from Judgment to the Love of God*. Grand Rapids: Baker, 2004.

Bruner, Frederick Dale. *The Christbook: Matthew 1–12*. Grand Rapids: Eerdmans, 1987.

Carson, D. A. *The Farewell Discourse and the Final Prayer of Jesus*. Grand Rapids: Baker, 1988.

Dorsett, Lyle W. *Seeking the Secret Place: The Spiritual Formation of C. S. Lewis*. Grand Rapids: Baker, 2004.

Duvall, J. Scott, and J. Daniel Hays. *Grasping God's Word: A Hands-On Approach to Reading, Interpreting, and Applying the Bible*. 2nd ed. Grand Rapids: Zondervan, 2005.

Edwards, Dwight. *Revolution Within: A Fresh Look at Supernatural Living*. New York: Random House, 2001.

Erickson, Millard J. *Christian Theology*. 2nd ed. Grand Rapids: Baker, 1998.

———. *The Concise Dictionary of Christian Theology*. Wheaton: Crossway, 2001.

Foster, Richard J. *Celebration of Discipline*. 25th anniversary ed. San Francisco: HarperSanFrancisco, 2003.

———. *Prayer: Finding the Heart's True Home*. San Francisco: HarperSanFrancisco, 1992.

Frazee, Randy. *The Connecting Church*. Grand Rapids: Zondervan, 2001.

Garland, David E. *Mark*. NIV Application Commentary. Grand Rapids: Zondervan, 1996.

Giglio, Louie. *The Air I Breathe: Worship as a Way of Life*. Sisters, OR: Multnomah, 2003.

Graham, Billy. *The Holy Spirit*. Dallas: Word, 1988.

Gray, Alice, ed. *Stories for the Heart: Over 100 Stories to Encourage Your Soul*. Sisters, OR: Multnomah, 1996.

Green, Michael. *Evangelism in the Early Church*. Rev. ed. Grand Rapids: Eerdmans, 2003.

Guinness, Os. *The Call: Finding and Fulfilling the Central Purpose of Your Life*. Nashville: Word, 1998.

Hendricks, Howard G., and William D. Hendricks. *Living By the Book*. Revised and expanded. Chicago: Moody, 2007.

Hoehner, Harold W. *Ephesians*. Grand Rapids: Baker, 2002.

Hughes, Kent. *Acts: The Church Afire*. Wheaton: Crossway, 1996.

Kallenberg, Brad. *Live to Tell: Evangelism to a Postmodern Age*. Grand Rapids: Brazos Press, 2002.

Keener, Craig S. *A Commentary on the Gospel of Matthew*. Grand Rapids: Eerdmans, 1999.

———. *Three Crucial Questions About the Holy Spirit*. Grand Rapids: Baker, 1996.

Kidner, Derek. *Genesis*. Tyndale Old Testament Commentary. Downers Grove, IL: InterVarsity Press, 1982.

Larson, Craig Brian, ed. *Choice Contemporary Stories and Illustrations for Preachers, Teachers, and Writers*. Grand Rapids: Baker, 1998.

———. *Illustrations for Preaching and Teaching*. Grand Rapids: Baker, 1993.

Laubach, Frank. *Letters by a Modern Mystic*. Westwood, NJ: Revell, 1958.

Lewis, C. S. *The Four Loves*. Glasgow: William Collins, 1960.

———. *The Great Divorce*. New York: Macmillan, 1946.

———. *Letters to Malcolm Chiefly on Prayer*. New York: Harcourt, 1964.

———. *Mere Christianity*. New York: Macmillan, 1952.

———. *The Screwtape Letters*. New York: Macmillan, 1961.

———. *The Weight of Glory*. 1949. San Francisco: HarperSanFrancisco, 1980.

Liefeld, Walter L. "Luke" in *Expositor's Bible Commentary*, vol. 8, ed. Frank E. Gaebelein. Grand Rapids: Zondervan, 1984.

Long, Jimmy. *Emerging Hope: Strategy for Reaching Postmodern Generations*. 2nd ed. Downers Grove, IL: InterVarsity Press, 2004.

Lucado, Max. *The Great House of God*. Dallas: Word, 1997.

Manning, Brennan. *The Wisdom of Tenderness: What Happens When God's Fierce Mercy Transforms Our Lives*. San Francisco: Harper San Francisco, 2004.

McGrath, Alister E. *Understanding the Trinity*. Grand Rapids: Zondervan, 1988.

Miller, Don. *Blue Like Jazz: Nonreligious Thoughts on Christian Spirituality*. Thorndike, ME: Thorndike, 2006.

Moltmann, Jürgen. *Theology of Hope*. Minneapolis: Fortress, 1993.

Moo, Douglas J. *Romans*. NIV Application Commentary. Grand Rapids: Zondervan, 2000.

Murray, Andrew. *With Christ in the School of Prayer*. Grand Rapids: Revell, 1895.

Nouwen, Henri J. M. *The Only Necessary Thing*. New York: Crossroad, 1999.

Olson, Roger E. *The Mosaic of Christian Belief*. Downers Grove, IL: InterVarsity Press, 2002.

Ortberg, John. *Everybody's Normal Till You Get to Know Them*. Grand Rapids: Zondervan, 2003.

———. *The Life You've Always Wanted*. Grand Rapids: Zondervan, 1997.

———. *Love Beyond Reason: Moving God's Love From Your Head to Your Heart*. Grand Rapids: Zondervan, 1998.

———. "Spiritual Growth—My Job or God's?" Preaching Today tape #190, at www.preachingtoday sermons.com.

Pate, C. Marvin et al. *The Story of Israel: A Biblical Theology*. Downers Grove, IL: InterVarsity Press, 2004.

Piper, John. *Let the Nations Be Glad: The Supremacy of God in Missions*. 2nd ed. Rev. and exp. Grand Rapids: Baker, 2003.

Plantinga, Cornelius. *Not the Way It's Supposed to Be: A Breviary of Sin*. Grand Rapids: Eerdmans, 1995.

Press, Bill. *Spin This: All the Ways We Don't Tell the Truth*. New York: Simon and Schuster, 2002.

Roberts, Mark D. *Dare to Be True: Living in the Freedom of Complete Honesty*. Colorado Springs: Waterbrook, 2003.

Shelley, Bruce L. *Theology for Ordinary People: What You Should Know to Make Sense Out of Life*. Downers Grove, IL: InterVarsity Press, 1993.

Sider, Ronald J. *Good News and Good Works*. Grand Rapids: Baker, 1993.

Sittser, Gerald L. *The Will of God as a Way of Life: Finding and Following the Will of God*. Grand Rapids: Zondervan, 2000.

Smedes, Lewis B. *The Art of Forgiving*. New York: Random House, 1997.

Smith, Gordon T. *The Voice of Jesus: Discernment, Prayer, and the Witness of the Spirit*. Downers Grove, IL: InterVarsity Press, 2003.

Stott, John R. W. *Authentic Christianity: From the Writings of John Stott*. Ed. Timothy Dudley-Smith. Downers Grove, IL: InterVarsity Press, 1996.

———. *Basic Christianity*. Grand Rapids: Eerdmans, 1986.

———. *The Cross of Christ*. Downers Grove, IL: InterVarsity Press, 1986.

———. *The Message of Galatians*. The Bible Speaks Today. Downers Grove, IL: InterVarsity Press, 1968.

———. *The Message of the Sermon on the Mount*. The Bible Speaks Today. Downers Grove, IL: InterVarsity Press, 1978.

Swenson, Richard A. *Margin*. Colorado Springs: NavPress, 1992.

Tabb, Mark. *Mission to Oz: Reaching Postmoderns Without Losing Your Way*. Chicago: Moody, 2004.

Thomas à Kempis. *Imitation of Christ*. Notre Dame, IN: Ave Maria Press, 1989.

Warren, Rick. *The Purpose-Driven Life*. Grand Rapids: Zondervan, 2002.

WORKS CITED

Webster, Doug. *The Easy Yoke.* Colorado Springs: NavPress, 1995.

Wilkins, Michael J. *Following the Master: A Biblical Theology of Discipleship.* Grand Rapids: Zondervan, 1992.

————. *In His Image: Reflecting Christ in Everyday Life.* Colorado Springs: NavPress, 1997.

————. *Matthew.* NIV Application Commentary. Grand Rapids: Zondervan, 2004.

Willard, Dallas. *Renovation of the Heart.* Colorado Springs: NavPress, 2002.

————. *The Spirit of the Disciplines.* San Francisco: HarperSanFrancisco, 1988.

Yancey, Philip. *Church: Why Bother?* Grand Rapids: Zondervan, 1998.

————. *The Jesus I Never Knew.* Grand Rapids: Zondervan, 1995.

J Scott Duvall is professor of New Testament at Ouachita Baptist University, a Christian liberal-arts college in Arkansas, where he teaches Spiritual Formation, Interpreting the Bible, Greek, and New Testament Studies. He received his B.A. from Ouachita and his M.Div. and Ph.D. from Southwestern Seminary, and has been teaching at OBU since 1989.

He also serves as copastor of Fellowship Church of Arkadelphia, Arkansas, where part of his ministry is to write resources such as *Experiencing God's Story of Life and Hope: A Workbook for Spiritual Formation*.

Duvall's other publications include *Grasping God's Word, Journey into God's Word, Preaching God's Word, Biblical Greek Exegesis, The Story of Israel,* and *The Dictionary of Biblical Prophecy and End Times*.